SOME EXPERIMENTS IN FOUR-DIMENSIONAL VISION

BY

GEOFFREY HODSON

AND

ALEXANDER HORNE

LONDON: RIDER & CO.
PATERNOSTER HOUSE, E.C.

Made and Printed in Great Britain at
The Mayflower Press, Plymouth. William Brendon & Son, Ltd.
1933

INTRODUCTION

WHEN Sir William Crookes, in violation of one of those unwritten laws which appear to have governed the scientists of the Victorian era, attempted to apply the scientific method to the examination of so-called psychical phenomena, he was persecuted and abused by his professional confrères. *The impassioned refusal of the orthodox scientists of that day to acknowledge even the existence of phenomena of this order is now not difficult to understand: there was no place for them in the framework of physics as it existed at that time. Anything in the nature of an astral visitant or other ghostly presence, like rodents or termites in the framework of a building, would have imperilled the structure which these men had built up and were solicitous to maintain; so they treated Crookes as a renegade and a traitor when he refused to unite with them in keeping these pests out.*

But had they only known it, the real threat to their neat theories lay in quite a different direction, which happened to be the very one which they themselves were pursuing with such single-minded ardour. For the thing which has caused the downfall of classical physics and has brought science to the very threshold of mysticism is nothing other than its own natural and normal advance along lines chosen by itself, and within its own self-constituted field of endeavour. Radioactivity, quanta, space-time, have proven to be spectres far more dangerous and devastating to time-honoured concepts than any harmless ghosts evoked by Crookes. We are too near this great reversal—for that's what it amounts to—to comprehend its full import or know whither it may lead, but this much at least is certain : it has put an end to dogmatism and has given immensely more " room to move about." In the new framework of physics there is even room for that order of phenomena which Crookes essayed to explore, and it is the fascination of the new science that nobody now knows what discoveries lie just around the corner.

One thing which sharply differentiates the new theoretical physics from the old—Einstein's from Newton's—is the idea of the nature of space and time. Space is now conceived of as n*-dimensional, with time as its fourth dimension. Mathematical physicists discovered that experimental contradictions disappeared if, instead of referring* *phenomena to a set of three space axes and one time axis of reference, they referred them to a set of four interchangeable axes involving four homogeneous co-ordinates. In other words, they used time exactly as though it were a dimension of space, because the clock could replace the tape-measure or the tape-measure the clock with equal facility. This means that space is (at least) four dimensional, and that idea forms an inexpugnable part of the theory of relativity. From far back the* mathematical *reality of the fourth and higher dimensions has never been in question, but with their entrance into physical theory the query inevitably arises: Are there "worlds" corresponding to these higher dimensions—is there any body for this mathematical soul?*

There is a growing conviction in certain quarters that there must be, and one indication lies in the fact that certain psychic phenomena (which since Crookes' day have enormously increased in volume) are explicable on this hypothesis. If, for the geometrico-mathematical definition of phenomena of this order, a four-dimensional system of co-ordinates is necessary, it is a natural inference that "the astral world" is four dimensional.

Any cogent argument or additional evidence, of any kind or from any source, to this effect is therefore very much in order. For this reason alone the present volume, " Some Experiments in Four-Dimensional Vision," should be welcomed. But it should be welcomed for another reason also : Ouspensky says, in " Tertium Organum," " In the world's literature there exist books usually little known. . . . These, taken together, will yield so clear and complete a picture of human existence, its path and goal, that there will be no further doubts about the destiny of humanity (though only in its minor part), but a destiny of quite a different sort from that which positive philosophy, ' historical materialism ' and ' socialism ' have in store for mankind." Now all of Geoffery Hodson's books belong to this category, and this one is no exception, even though its field is limited to the role of Mr. Hodson as " witness," with Mr. Horne playing the part of " examiner." It seems to me that both play their parts well, and that the thing which they have undertaken was well worth the doing, however lacking in finality ; for these are new fields which they essay to explore.

To anyone acquainted with Mr. Hodson, doubt of the genuineness of his clairvoyant power would be grotesque, for it is of such a nature as to convince the most sceptical ; but for the benefit of those who know nothing about him, and to whom the word " clairvoyance " connotes some kind of sporadic psychism or trance mediumship, I would say that his powers are of an altogether different order; that they were won by his own individual effort, maintained by a pure life and a strict regimen, and exercised only in the disinterested service of his fellow man.

CLAUDE BRAGDON.

NEW YORK,
May 21, 1933.

CONTENTS

PART I

PART II

CONTENTS

PART III

APPENDIX

LIST OF ILLUSTRATIONS

PREFACE

The Nature of Occult Research

To those unacquainted with the character of Mr. Hodson's work in the domain of occult research, it is necessary to preface the discussion of his investigations with a few remarks on the subject of "positive" and "negative" clairvoyance.

Negative Clairvoyance

Negative clairvoyance is the type of "second sight" found in some mediums, in some psychopathic patients, and occasionally in sensitive children. Its manifestation is sporadic in character (hence its "negative" designation), coming and going without warning, and altogether beyond the control of the subject. It may appear only at one period in life, as at childhood, for example, and then disappear for ever. Or it may come to the surface out of the depths of the sub-conscious self during a temporary derangement or strain in the nervous or cerebral system, disappearing again when balance and normality have been restored. Or again, as in the case of mediums, a peculiar condition in the organism may keep it more or less open to the more delicate vibrations going on around us continually, which thus enables them to " hear " or " see " things to which the more normal person is impervious.[1]

That the above, generally speaking, represents the true state of affairs is a commonplace of modern psychology. Many staid and respectable scientists have staked their reputations and standing in the professional world on the belief that the human psyche contains profundities beyond the reach of the more normal self, and the list of distinguished names that has graced the presidential chair of the Society for Psychical Research is eloquent testimony to this fact.[2] *All of them have testified to the existence in man of mysterious and abnormal faculties and powers, and the catalogue of manifestations—and the list of their supporters—is daily growing.*

Unfortunately, some investigators have taken the stand that these faculties—while genuine enough in themselves—are always *evidence of a*

---

[1] A favourite analogy is that of the radio receiver, which to-day registers vibrations that it was impossible to reproduce formerly. A " negative " receiver, however, would be one having no switch or tuning dial. It is thus always " open " and at the mercy of whatever happens to be " on the air." This no doubt goes far to explain the extreme banality of so many mediumistic " messages."

[2] Some of the more prominent might here be mentioned: Sir William Crookes; Professors Bergson, Driesch, and William James; Sir Oliver Lodge, Charles Richet, Flammarion, and a host of others.

derangement of the physiological or psychological mechanism. Max Nordau, for instance, has made a virulent attack on most forms of art and most manifestations of genius as being evidences of degeneration, and makes mystical and occult tendencies the special object of his vitriolic wrath. His book " Degeneration," however, is one-sided and to that extent untrue, in that it fails to take into account the healthy and normal and sane manifestations of the very same powers which, in unbalanced people, manifest themselves in an unbalanced manner.

Positive Clairvoyance

That abnormal powers exist in a balanced and healthy state (as well as in the opposite) is fortunately also true, and the catalogue of these *manifestations is also growing, though not at the same rate as the other, previously mentioned; perhaps because the conditions to be fulfilled are more stringent; perhaps also because those who are possessed of them do not (like so many mediums) flaunt their possessions before the world. They on the contrary have to be sought out in most cases, and when so sought out, usually display a modesty and reticence which are perhaps the best evidence of the unpretentiousness of their powers.*

Some of our leading thinkers of to-day have not hesitated to attest their belief in the genuineness of this fairly prevalent phenomenon. Thus P. D. Ouspensky, in his latest work, " A New

Model of the Universe," *points out that* "*the psychological study of man has recognised the reality of states of consciousness which were long considered pathological, and has admitted their cognitive value, that is to say, the fact that in these states of consciousness man is able to know what he cannot know in ordinary states.*"[1]

Similarly Count Hermann Keyserling, in his "*Travel Diary of a Philosopher,*" *discussing the merits of occultism's claims, maintains that* "*anyone, who, like myself, takes the trouble to study them seriously, will come to the conclusion that it is not all imaginary; that the possibility of much of it is certain, and the reality probable.*" *The world of which we are normally conscious, he says, is only a section of reality. Alter the consciousness, and our perceptual world changes. Furthermore, if you extend the boundaries of your consciousness, your world correspondingly begins to manifest laws and forces that were not heretofore apparent.*[2]

There certainly does seem to be very good evidence, coming from creditable sources, and corroborated in many departments of science and thought, that the objective universe is more extensive than is apparent to our normal senses, and that, deep in the structure of man's consciousness, there exist faculties corresponding to cosmic

---

[1] *Op. cit.*, p. 17.
[2] *Op. cit.*, chapter on "Adyar."

levels beyond the purely physical. The ability to receive visual impressions of some of these levels is what we call clairvoyance. When it is more or less under control, when the subject retains full physical consciousness during its use, together with the normal faculties of judgment, clear thinking, and healthy and balanced physiological functioning, it is called "positive" clairvoyance. When on the contrary, as we have already pointed out, it is spasmodic, or entails a partial or total loss of consciousness on the part of the subject, with abnormal physiological manifestations such as irregular breathing, convulsions, etc., it is called "negative" clairvoyance. The latter form is discouraged by theosophical thinkers and investigators, and any method of self-development that leads to this subnormal and unhealthy condition is stigmatized as being unworthy of the genuine aspirant, to whom a supernormal but perfectly healthy and balanced method of self-training (less popular with some because it is slower and more strenuous) is always open.

Evidences of Mr. Hodson's Clairvoyant Power

That Mr. Hodson has developed the faculty of positive clairvoyance to a remarkable degree those who know him well have no doubt. In "The Science of Seership," one of his collaborators records a series of experiments with bar magnets and test-tubes containing some of the gaseous chemical elements. In the latter instance, Mr. Hodson found it possible to describe the atomic structure of these gaseous bodies by clairvoyant means, and, by checking back with such works as "Occult Chemistry,"[1] *the accuracy of his clairvoyant power was established (incidentally corroborating, on a scientific basis, the correctness of the descriptions given in the latter work).*

In the case of the bar magnet, Mr. Hodson found it possible (by purely visual means) to distinguish the north and south poles and the flow of magnetic emanation, something normally impossible. Similarly, in a forthcoming work on occult astro-physics at present in manuscript form, Mr. Hodson records a series of investigations of the planetary positions (again by clairvoyant means) which, when checked by the usual astronomical tables, were found to be accurate in a large majority of instances.[2]

In an article on "The Occult Side of Disease,"[3] *Dr. W. M. Davidson (a non-Theosophist) records a number of experiments and investigations*

---

[1] By Dr. Annie Besant and C. W. Leadbeater. In this work the atomic structure of the chemical elements is given as seen by occult vision.

[2] It is only fair to add that, in these experiments, the clairvoyant observations were in a few instances not correct. Mr. Hodson records the incorrect with the correct cases, the proportion of the latter being very much greater than could be accounted for by the Law of Probabilities.

[3] *World Theosophy*, March, 1932.

carried on by Mr. Hodson in the former's presence, in collaboration with a number of other physicians, in which the investigator's clairvoyant power came on many occasions objectively into evidence, beyond shadow of a doubt.

In a study of certain homeopathic remedies, for instance, "the reality of clairvoyance was again demonstrated," says Dr. Davidson, "for Mr. Hodson, who was obviously most imperfectly acquainted with these remedies, again and again correctly enumerated the known qualities of the specimens submitted, and discerned their already ascertained powers with a swiftness which was amazing."

In an investigation covering the mechanism of the so-called Electronic Reactions of Abrams, to give still another example, Dr. Davidson speaks of the "very remarkable way in which Mr. Hodson repeatedly discerned the exact area of 'dullness' on the abdomen of the subject long before the doctor got it by means of his rod."

During these and many other investigations carried out by this group, Dr. Davidson tells us that he was "in the fortunate position of being able to 'check' many of the results in a way Mr. Hodson was scarcely aware of. . . . For example, in an effort to scientifically 'check' the results, I asked Dr. Grimmer to supply me with a number of vials of the homeopathic remedies marked only with numbers, so that even I would not know what the drugs were. On commencing with these,

Mr. Hodson expressed a desire to know at least what remedies they were. I was unable to tell, but offered to telephone Dr. Grimmer to find out. He was not available, so without further ado Mr. Hodson started to 'look' them over. After only a few seconds observation he picked out one of the twenty-five vials and said, 'This is the most active one in the group,' and later that evening Dr. Grimmer confirmed that that was indeed one of the highest potencies present—the 50*M. Anyone acquainted with homeopathy will need no emphasis of the magnitude of that achievement. . . .*

"*Another incident worthy of note: On one occasion it was thought desirable to test some of the remedies on my own etheric double. On looking into my hand to estimate my 'etheric rate' he at once exclaimed, 'How slow and sluggish your etheric currents are.' To anyone who knows how laborious and troublesome it is to make a B.M.R. (Basal Metabolism Rate estimation) of a patient, such an instant perception was an extraordinary achievement, especially as I knew in various ways that I* do *have a somewhat sub-normal metabolism.*"

In the investigation of disease-conditions themselves (physical or mental), "*the instantaneity with which Mr. Hodson perceived the inmost nature of a patient was truly remarkable. In those cases where the patients were intimately known to me (Mr. Hodson knew absolutely nothing whatever about them until they sat down before him), his ability to recognize and understand some of their subtlest characteristics would make any psycho-analyst most envious. . . . Many other 'unconscious' proofs of the reality of the inner vision were afforded as we went along."*

It is this same "inner vision" that Mr. Hodson has turned on the question of four-dimensional space and its characteristics. During the course of these experiments also, several corroborative circumstances cropped up, as in Dr. Davidson's case. These evidences will be noted in the records as we proceed.

The main purpose of these experiments, however, was, not to check up on Mr. Hodson's supernormal faculties (which were taken as having already been established), but to check up on our mathematical conception of hyper-space, and to see whether, by any chance, direct clairvoyant observation could not furnish us with any positive information (corroborative or otherwise) regarding some of our speculations concerning the fourth dimension. With two notable exceptions, no experimental verification had so far been attempted in the direction of establishing a definite connection between mathematical theory and clairvoyant investigation. These two exceptions are :

1. *the descriptions that Johann van Manen has given of things seen four-dimensionally, in his*

"Some Occult Experiences"—chance experiences rather than experiments in the true sense;

2. the statements that C. W. Leadbeater has made with respect to his own astral vision and four-dimensional theory, definitely linking the two together.[1]

From the theoretical standpoint, the subject has already been treated in my "Theosophy and the Fourth Dimension."

It was thought, however, that if an investigation were carried out with the definite object of ascertaining what connection there might actually be between astral vision and the four-dimensional theory, it might lead to interesting results. A series of experiments was accordingly undertaken by Mr. Hodson with this object in view, and recorded verbatim by myself, later analysing the descriptions given, from the four-dimensional standpoint. The present work is a record of both the verbatim notes and their mathematical interpretation. If both seem at times to be tedious and pedantic, our only excuse is that we are here blazing a new trail in four-dimensional thought, and it was thought better to record every statement and its possible mathematical interpretation, for study and consideration by the individual student, rather than present a series of more or less

[1] *e.g.* " . . . for astral sight, the theory of the Fourth Dimension gives a neater and more complete explanation." *The Astral Plane*, p. 24.

superficial deductions, without the actual material on which these deductions were based.

As we have remarked in "Suggestions for further research," it is hoped that others will be induced to continue this line of investigation along some of the paths laid down.

A. HORNE.

PART I

RECORD OF THE FIRST EXPERIMENT

Place: San Francisco, U.S.A.

Time: September 28, 1931. 4 to 5 p.m.

Object examined: A wooden cube taken from a child's toy-box; size, seven-eighths of an inch to the edge. On one face the number 13 had been inscribed in pencil, and in the examination this face was held away from the observer, right-side up.

No attempts were made to direct the examination during the first experiment, it being thought best simply to make a record of whatever Mr. Hodson chanced to see, if anything. One question, however, was asked at the beginning: "Can you see the number 13? Does it appear as if the cube were transparent and you were looking through to the other end, or as if the cube were turned around, facing you?" This question was not answered till about the middle of the experiment (see lines 70–74, below). Its significance is discussed in Part II.

Details of the manner in which the experiments were conducted will no doubt be of interest. Mr. Hodson would place the cube to his forehead, holding it between his two hands, and through closed eyes would perform the examination. Normal physical consciousness was retained throughout ; voice, mannerisms, etc., were not any different from what

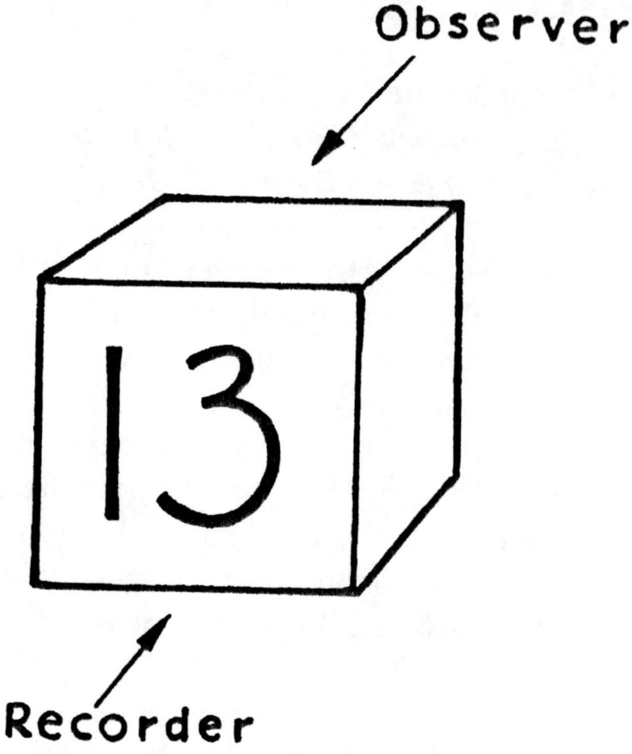

Fig. 1

they might have been had the observer been looking through a microscope or other scientific instrument ; no nervous tension, irritability, or hyper-sensitiveness noted as usually reported in spiritualistic séances. Examination and description were punctuated here and there by conversation between observer and recorder.

The examination was performed in daylight, with the shades drawn.

Mr. Hodson, after a minute or so of quiet concentration, began to report as follows:

" My first experience is within the limits of physical perspective. I am looking into the cube as into a corridor; I can see the other end, apparently smaller than my end. The vision here used is the lowest kind of etheric vision and I am deliberately inhibiting flights of consciousness into higher levels.

My next impression is that of being in the centre of the cube, which is now of enormous dimensions, and which has now become a perfect cube [whereas it was at first seen in perspective]. It is seen from within, all the sides being equal and all angles right-angles; all are perceived at once, without the necessity of turning around. This is still etheric vision, but of a slightly higher order. I do not now see the outside of the cube.

I have now distinct triple consciousness, consisting of:

i. Part of my consciousness, which is within the cube.

ii. The rest of my bodily consciousness, with which I can see clairvoyantly the projection of myself in the cube, and its size relative to the cube, which is about one-fifth in height [relative to the cube].

iii. Consciousness of a universal super-awareness centred in my ego ; a watching consciousness.

I perceive that the cube has extensions with vision (i), and with vision (ii) I see the extensions. There are diagonal extensions of all edges from the centre of the cube. Each of these extensions is a shimmering whitish blue light, and there are cross-connections linking the extended edges.

There is suddenly a change ; I am looking into the middle of the extended figure, resembling a spider's web in three dimensions. Further complications are noticed : edges also are extended along the direction of the sides, with the same phenomena of light and linking. I find it difficult to hold the two kinds of vision (i) and (ii) at the same time.

Two major cross-sections suddenly interpose themselves as an extended diagonal cross [here Mr. Hodson makes a motion with his finger like the letter 'X']. This vision increases ; the whole cube looks and feels to my hands as a pulsing, living entity, a kind of engine. Vision is rendered difficult at this point by sudden appearance of cross-sections at different angles, both of the extended figure and physical cube.

No unification possible with this type of vision, which is still etheric. An extremely intricate network of lines is formed, reminding me of closely drawn tangential lines to a circle in opposite directions, criss-crossing; these are lines of force, with energy definitely running along them.

The point-consciousness (i) inside the cube perceives a transparent darkness through which the insides loom like the walls of an enormous square room, but dark.

The '3' in the figure '13' written on the far-side of the cube appears with vision (ii) to be on the right. [Later, Mr. Hodson described the appearance of the '3' as being normal, instead of reversed.][1]

I have now raised the order of vision to the astro-etheric, a little of both. The first peculiarity is the appearance of a large letter 'U'; in cross-section this would be a square. The cube itself is at the bottom of the 'U,' which passes through the right and left sides. The same phenomenon has occurred with the other sides. Two 'U's' are seen; [later seen as being but one 'U,' seen differently].

The inter-section of the two 'U's' makes the visible cube. They have colour; a

---

[1] See Fig 1.

sort of yellow-orange. The cube is inseparable from them, and extensible into them with this vision. The limitation in size, physically, seems very arbitrary.
With higher vision, an extension of (ii), the ' U's ' vanish and the sides extend into a figure apparently infinite on all the sides; a series of crosses without beginning. This is still spatial and more or less three-dimensional. I have a sense of looking down into the physical cube which is black, while all around are the extensions of yellowish light. All the arms fade and shade off, losing their colour and edge rather vaguely in this pit of darkness. Each of these six arms are lines of force, forces rushing through them at a tremendous pace. I have a curious sense of infinity and eternity with respect to these arms and forces, which contain all the possible directions in which ' U's ' can be drawn."

A curious experience that Mr. Hodson reported was that the physical cube could not be seen at the same time as the super-physical " U." Focussing the consciousness on one seemed to shut out the other instantly. The physical cube, moreover, felt to Mr. Hodson to be a cramped limitation in comparison to the " U," which was ever so much freer and limitless. A sensation of exhilaration seemed to accompany the contemplation of the superphysical extension of the cube, a sense of being in the presence of universals, rather than of particular forms. An extreme difficulty was at all times experienced in choosing appropriate words to describe the things seen.

RECORD OF THE SECOND EXPERIMENT

Time: October 9, 1931. 2.45 p.m.
Object examined: The Cube, as previously.
Mr. Hodson's verbatim report is as follows:

"Clairvoyant sight of the cube adds the following new impressions to it:

(*a*) Motion in two directions; an expansion consisting of an outflow of energy, chiefly on the lines of the edges and giving the impression of infinity, *i.e.* as far as one can keep in touch with the cube and look outwards.

(*b*) Transparency, giving a crystalline appearance.

(*c*) Luminosity, giving colour.

(*d*) Possibility of projecting the consciousness into the cube and looking at it as if from within, the size of the cube being colossal. I cannot look out beyond the cube."

Notes taken at the time (but not verbatim) disclose the following additional information:

Asked whether the outflowing lines in the diagram (Fig. 4) were as drawn (*i.e.* at an angle of approximately forty-five degrees), or whether they actually were at right angles to the three dimensions of the physical cube, Mr. Hodson replied that the impression he had, when observing the corner point of the cube, for instance, was of a line moving inwards, rather than in the exact manner shown in the diagram; moreover, this motion inwards was accomplished without losing sight of the point of the cube itself, a seeming paradox, for motion was accomplished without actually moving away from the starting-point. I gave an analogy from the two and three-dimensional point of view, using a plane of glass and a square to depict the analogous situation, and Mr. Hodson expressed himself as satisfied that the analogy correctly described the situation as he saw it.[1]

Asked whether he could now see the number "13,"[2] he replied that the "3" was on his right, and reversed. He, however, spoke of it as the number "31."

Asked whether he could make himself see the "13" correctly [*i.e.* as if the number were facing him, right-side up] he said that after an effort he could do so, but it required a great effort of will, and

---

[1] See Figs. 8 and 9 and "Remarks on the Second Experiment." [2] See Fig. 2.

something seemed to be pulling him back to the other position; vision seemed to have a kind of elasticity. [Mr. Hodson seemed somewhat tired during these experiments.]

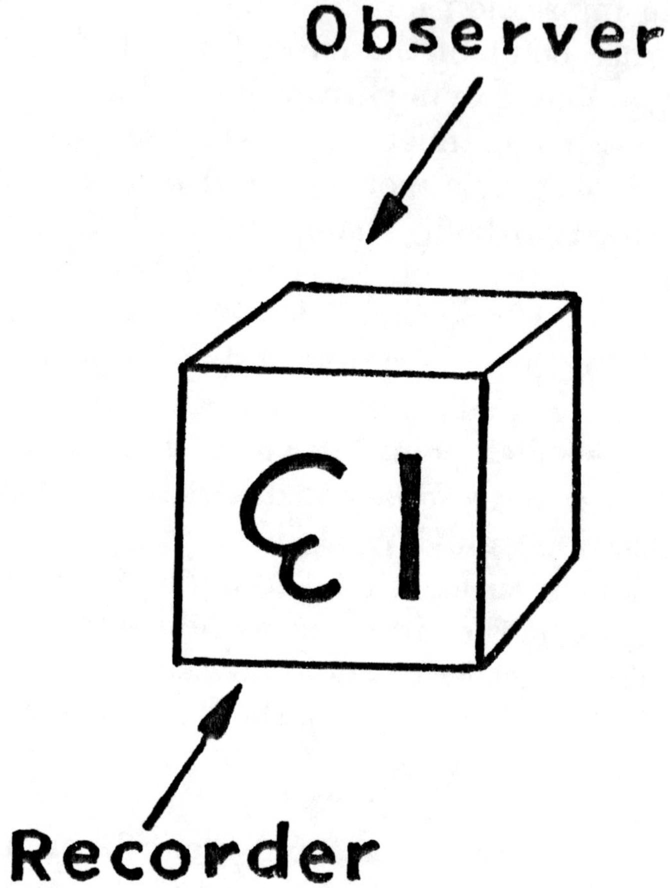

Fig. 2

The cube, upon further examination seemed to extend outwards and inwards both; infinitely outwards, and coming to a point inwards. Being shown Fig. 22 in my book *Theosophy and the Fourth Dimension*, Mr.

Hodson stated that the figure was a correct representation of what he saw in regard to this inward-outward progression of the cube. Upon the assumption (borne out by four-dimensional reasoning) that this inward-outward progression was an optical illusion, brought about by four-dimensional perspective, and that the inward progression never really ended in a point (just as the apparently-converging tracks of a railway never really end in a point) Mr. Hodson said that, upon closer examination, that was correct. He never really lost sight of the form of a cube, and the inward-outward progression was always in the shape of a cube, the manner of progression being parallel rather than converging (to use the railway-track analogy). The cube-form, in progressing inwards, did not seem to grow smaller (though it at first seemed to do so, ending in a point).

RECORD OF THE THIRD EXPERIMENT

Time: October 23, 1931. 3.0 p.m.
Object examined: The cube.

This experiment, which was of short duration, was directed toward the elucidation of several problems raised by the previous investigations. It therefore took the form of a series of questions and answers.

1. Question: "Is the radiation purely an extension of the edges, as previously reported, or does the space enclosed by the radiating planes appear to be filled in with some sort of substance?"
Answer: "Examining one side to seek an answer, I see, first, the pyramid already described.[1] Focussing my attention on the plane surface as distinct from the edges,[2] I see an infinite number of pyramids;[3] *i.e.* they appear to be pyramids, as extensions of every possible square that could be drawn on the surface. Wherever

---

[1] See Fig. 4. A series of six pyramidical forms appears to radiate out from the centre of the cube. *b–p*, *c–n*, *g–q*, and *f–r*, is one of them.

[2] The surface *bfcg*, for instance.

[3] See Fig. 10.

I fix my attention, on that plane there is a pyramid. I cannot see them all at once, with astral vision, but only the major one formed by the real edges, and one other, at any point that I will; so that I still get the effect of the extension of lines, as long as I limit myself to the vision which shows extension of edges.

“Looking down into the pyramid, it appears hollow, and by looking down into it I perceive that it is not a pyramid but an extended square. Immediately I withdraw the point of vision from within the extended lines, looking from outside, then perspective demands the pyramid-shape.

“Even if I deliberately focus on a point on the surface, the appearance of a minute pyramid is seen.

“Looking down, the sense of motion is accentuated, as if the whole side were coming up towards me, going through my head and past me into infinite space.”

2. Question: “Is the cross-form (Fig. 7) created by the extended planes, only another view of the diagonal extensions, seen from another angle perhaps, or does it comprise a totally different and independent figure?”

Answer: “The extensions of the sides appear to be composed of forces moving towards the cube. At least, movement in that direction is accentuated; whereas in the other (*i.e.* the extended edges), movement away from the cube is accentuated, as far as vision is concerned." In other words, there is an outrush of force in the case of the edge-extended figure (Fig. 4), and an inrush in the case of the cross, or side-extended figure (Fig. 7).

3. Question: "Is it not possible that the cross-form is an etheric counterpart of the cube, whereas the edge-extended figure is astral?"

Answer: "With etheric vision you see chiefly the atomic discharges, which form a kind of haze which tends to become spherical," forming a kind of spherical aura. "Inside, intense molecular and atomic activity becomes visible, the whole cube boiling, as it were, somewhat as the Brownian movement in colloidal solutions. This is all due to the inrush and arrival, at the etheric level, of force. It is an interior welling up, rather than a passage through the edges.

"The first phenomenon as astral vision is turned on, is of the extended edges, and that is the true astral description of the cube.

"Evidently there are sub-plane correspondences, in each plane, to each of the major seven planes; *i.e.* the Causal plane impinges on the astral, at, say, the fifth sub-plane, and sight on that sub-plane tends to let in Causal conceptions. Indeed, they would automatically come in as the sight was raised to that sub-plane. If the seer's consciousness is limited to, say, the Causal, he would find it somewhat difficult to penetrate past the corresponding sub-plane, the phenomenon there arresting his attention, with a sense of finality or ultimateness.

" Both the ' U ' and the cross are explainable on these grounds. The cross has no real existence. It is a description under the limitations of perspective, and forms but one aspect of the archetypal cube.

" The cross and the ' U ' are cross-sections of the causal cube," and are but two aspects of perhaps an infinite series of possibilities, whereas the edge-extended figure has independent, objective reality.

4. Question : " What are the cross-connections and linkages spoken of in connection with the description of the edge-extended figure ? "

Answer : " They are planes connecting the extended edges, forming an apparently infinite series of squares spreading outwards from the centre."

RECORD OF THE FOURTH EXPERIMENT

Time: October 31, 1931. 2.30 p.m.
Objects examined: (1) A cube, as before.
(2) A book.

1. Question: "Looking at one of the extending cubes reported in the Third Experiment, is it actually hollow, or only seemingly so; does it seem to have at least the same degree of solidity as the physical cube has, when seen with astral vision?"
Answer: "There are two situations: one is that I can concentrate on one square to such an extent that I do not see the interior ones, and that gives the appearance of hollowness. . . . Yes, it is actually a perfect hollow—a state of negation. If I diffuse my sight, I can still hold that square as the outstanding one, but the rest of the cube is filled with a whitish haze in great molecular and atomic activity. . . . Now I have succeeded in keeping the inner square hollow and can see the space between it and the edge-cube filled in. . . . Yes, it is a fullness, but there is a tendency for the vision to fix itself on the sides of the cube and not see the interior."

2. Question : " Looking at the closed book before you, first with etheric and then with astral vision, what is the principle difference noticed as between these two types of vision ? "

Answer : " With etheric vision, the first phenomenon is Radiation—a greyish blue haze surrounding the whole book, and within the book, but the particles much closer together in the latter case, giving the appearance of much greater density.

" The second phenomenon is Movement—the etheric double of the book is just very slightly moving, in contrast to the immovable stability of the physical book. An emanation from the ink and gum [glue] can be observed, differing from the emanation from the paper. The text of the book is seen as an interlocking fretwork.

" With astral vision, an aura is seen, extending about six inches all around the book; gives me a sense of being alive, an entity with individuality. It has life and a thought-atmosphere about it which is apparent even at the lowest astral sub-plane; it has a character of its own. With astral vision you contact the life-side of the book."

3. Question : " How does the printing look to you now ? "

Answer : " It looks as if it is upside-down."

[Correct.] "There is no fret-work; what letters I see are seen clearly, without the interlocking effect."

4. Question: "Can you see the printing right-side up?"

Answer: "Yes; the moment you mentioned it, the printing appeared right-side up instantaneously."

5. Question: "Going back to etheric vision, can you see the printing both upside-down and right-side up alternately?"

(Mr. Hodson made several attempts, but finally had to give it up. The printing continued to look upside-down to him even when he tried to place himself mentally in my position, sitting opposite him.)

RECORD OF THE FIFTH EXPERIMENT

Time : November 14, 1931. 2.30 p.m.

The purpose of this experiment was to investigate the problem of Time as a fourth dimension, as distinct from the previous experiments in the realm of Space. For this purpose, Mr. Hodson took his own physical body for the object of examination, and reported the following clairvoyant observations :

" The first sensation is that of following lines of force inwards towards the interior of my body, as if the whole surface of the body were making a slow inward movement, much as the inflowing lines of the cube were making. As I follow this progression inwards, I have gone right back to babyhood. I notice a few outstanding periods—my football-playing days, for instance. At ten I must have been wearing knickerbockers. I see myself as a boy. The whole atmosphere of that life comes to me, particularly a school building . . . pear trees in blossom. . . . I evidently am now at the age of ten, but at first I went right on, continuing this inward extension . . . I see my boyhood when I had my first bicycle. . . .

" I can see myself as a baby, the body being apparently inside me. . . I am conscious also of the external extension, which must be the Future, which is pulling me all the time. . . .

" All the atmosphere and surroundings of the home of my birth crowd in upon me, everything looking enormous, the rooms looking like auditoriums of colossal dimensions. It is just after my birth. . . . It has now become summer. I notice the condition of the infant body, even to the curiously crinkly condition of the skin. A woman—a kind of woman who helped—is there—an old family servant."

" Looking at myself again, I lose all sense of time. I see myself not as Geoffrey Hodson ' now,' but as an entity that sums up within itself my forty-five years of life. I am the summation into one time of all the processes of birth and growth, preserved into a unity, each moment affecting every other moment "—a curious synthesis of all states and stages of growth from the moment of birth to the age of forty-five, all conditions rolled into a unity.

" Looking ' forward,' I see a kind of hourglass, the ' present ' being the narrow point joining the two horned sections, the ‘ past ’ being one opening, and the ‘ future ’ being the other ; they look equal, there being no difference in size or importance.

“ I get a continuation of the sense of extension, and something that feels like growth of stature, as if I had not been quite erect, and was now becoming so. This expresses itself more in terms of a change in consciousness, rather than a bodily change. I find a steady increase coming over me in the direction of positive control by the Will, a steady increase in power, force ; the physical body is slightly thinner and more ascetic-looking ; I find a much greater sense of a ‘ mission,’ as if something has been said to me to point out my mission, or I had had an expansion of consciousness which had clearly indicated to me my mission—this is about ten years ‘ forward.’

“ I can feel my aura—or rather, this physical extension of myself into the ‘ future ’—but there is actually no change in size. I can see a little loneliness, as if cut off from physical associates and movements, standing alone.”

Mr. Hodson spoke continually of a sense of physical reality about all that he saw ; it was not reminiscing, and it was not looking at a photographic record of something that once existed ; he seemed to be looking at the physical reality directly—it had all the reality of " present " physical objects. Discussing psychometry and the theory of akashic records, he was of the opinion that the akashic theory did not quite cover the case entirely, because of this sense of physical reality about all " past " events that he saw, as if they still existed. The " present physical reality " of the things seen was the predominating phenomenon of the entire observation.

Looking into the " future," a difficulty was experienced; it did not come with the spontaneity of the examination into the " past," the latter coming so rapidly that transcription *verbatim* became difficult. Mr. Hodson complained several times of a pressure about the head and a sense of strain; a tendency to lose consciousness that had to be continually fought. The sense of strain remained for several hours.

PART II

REMARKS ON THE FIRST EXPERIMENT

I NOW propose to analyse the observations as reported by Mr. Hodson, in terms of the four-dimensional theory. It will be shown that while the record contains elements that I have so far been unable to explain in such terms, and other elements which have yielded negative results, there is much nevertheless that has a very definite bearing on four-dimensional theory, corroborating it in many respects, and, in turn, capable of explanation in terms of four-dimensional theory better than in terms of any other hypothesis.

On the subject of the negative results mentioned above I will say that I brought to these experiments certain irrepressible prepossessions resulting from my previous researches in four-dimensional geometry, and I came prepared therefore to see these prepossessions corroborated. I came, for instance, fully prepared to hear Mr. Hodson describe a tesseract,[1] this being the simplest unit of four-space (just as the cube is the simplest unit of three-space), the tesseract being therefore (presumably) the

[1] See *Theosophy and the Fourth Dimension*, Fig. 19, p. 84.

four-dimensional counterpart of a physical cube, visible as such to clairvoyant sight. I was moreover prepared to hear Mr. Hodson report experiencing true four-directional extension, as he gazed at this four-dimensional figure. In both these particulars I was somewhat disappointed, though later analysis to some extent softened the edge of my disappointment. These " negative results " will be referred to again under their appropriate heading.

Now as to the positive results.

Lines 1–8. We begin first with " etheric " vision, as the lowest manifestation of a faculty that is just beginning to take us beyond the range of normal vision of the three-dimensional world, and we find that this type of vision confers upon the seer a species of X-ray sight, apparently making of the solid cube, in this case, an empty corridor. In the second experiment, the phenomenon is further described as one of " transparency, giving a crystalline appearance."[1] However, inasmuch as the " etheric " in the theosophical terminology is only a refined grade of physical matter, it is quite understandable that etheric vision would still be within the confines of perspective (as Mr. Hodson reports) and the farther face

[1] Like a block of very clear ice, for instance. See line 133.

of the cube consequently would look, quite naturally, smaller than the nearer face (line 4). The etheric, in other words, is still a world of three dimensions; and etheric vision, as reported by Mr. Hodson, is found to have none of the characteristics that we can definitely call four-dimensional. Its principal value to us at this stage is in leading up to an order of vision that is distinctly different; later we shall have occasion to point out experimentally the characteristic difference that exists between "etheric" (three-dimensional) and "astral" (four-dimensional) clairvoyance.[1]

Lines 9–19. Here we are introduced to vision of a higher order than the etheric. The illusion of perspective is completely gone—"all sides being equal and all angles [being] right-angles." All sides, again, are perceived simultaneously "without the necessity of turning around." This is a perfect description of four-dimensional vision, as Fig. 3 indicates.

Thus, Fig. 3 (*a*) shows how a transparent square would look to a two-dimensional microbe situated at *A*, and gazing in the direction *AB* with X-ray vision: the far end becomes foreshortened, and the right-angles become distorted into acute angles.

To a being gifted with three-dimensional sight, however, the square would appear as at

[1] See "Remarks on the Fourth Experiment," below.

(*b*), for here the consciousness would be poised in higher space, as at *C*, and from that vantage-point the entire square, inside and outside, would be simultaneously visible, each line in correct proportion and every angle a right-angle. The illusion of perspective here is completely gone.[1]

Notice also that in Fig. 3 (*a*) the side nearer the observer *A* would be called " front," and the opposite side, " back," whereas in (*b*) the words front, back, right, left, lose all significance and become purely arbitrary. All four sides are simultaneously seen " without the necessity of turning around," just as Mr. Hodson reports.

Now, all four-dimensional mathematics bases itself on the supposition that what is true of the relationship between the worlds of two and three dimensions is similarly true of the world of three and four dimensions; consequently, a being with consciousness poised in four-dimensional space would see a three-dimensional cube in exactly the same manner as a being poised in three-space would see a two-dimensional square. This would therefore make the order of vision here used, four-dimensional

---

[1] Point *C*, of course, has to be equidistant from all four corners in order to overcome the effect of perspective, a somewhat artificial condition actually fulfilled in the experiment, since Mr. Hodson speaks of apparently being in the " centre " of the cube.

and astral in character, rather than etheric, as Mr. Hodson says.

C. W. Leadbeater, for instance, in describing the phenomena of the astral plane, says that on that plane " an object is seen, as it were, from all sides at once, the inside of a solid being as plainly open to the view as the outside."[1] Similarly, " the sides of a glass cube would appear all equal, as they really are,

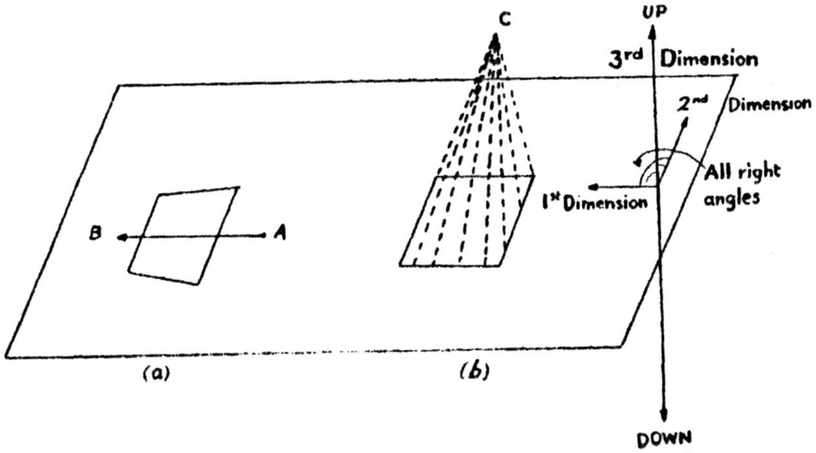

Fig. 3

while on the physical plane we see the further sides in perspective . . . smaller. . . . It is this characteristic of astral vision which has led to it sometimes being spoken of as sight in the Fourth Dimension—a very suggestive and expressive phrase."[2]

It is for this reason that I question whether Mr. Hodson is quite correct when he says that the faculty he was here using was " still etheric

[1] *The Astral Plane*, p. 12. [2] *Ibid.*, p. 19.

vision, but of a lightly higher order." I should say: of a vastly higher order—astral vision in short, taking one into an entirely different dimension.

The Magnifying Power of Clairvoyant Vision

In lines 20–29 we are introduced to an interesting phenomenon. Mr. Hodson here sees himself as a minute figure, apparently inside the cube, and one-fifth of its height. This would make his apparent height to be about one-sixth of an inch (since the cube was seven-eighths of an inch high). Taking his real height as five feet eight inches, this would be equivalent to reducing his mental image of himself 390 times, which again would have the effect of apparently increasing the size of the cube in the same proportion, since our notion of size is always purely relative.

The effect upon his consciousness at the time must therefore have been the same as if he had been standing in his normal physical body—poised in mid-air—in a room twenty-eight and a half feet in each dimension, the little cube assuming relatively those proportions. Hence his statement, "enormous dimensions" (line 10), and "enormous square room" (line 69). In the second experiment, he again refers to this phenomenon, where he speaks of "the size of the cube being colossal" (lines 138–139).

This phenomenon gives us one possible explanation of the faculty of clairvoyant magnification, referred to in various works by Dr. Besant, C. W. Leadbeater, C. Jinarajadasa, as well as Hodson. C. W. Leadbeater, for instance, compares this faculty of magnification to that conferred by a microscope, " though its magnifying power," he says, " is enormously greater than that of any microscope ever made or ever likely to be made."[1] The current occult explanation of such magnifying power is that a peculiar force emanates from the frontal *chakram*,[2] but just how such an emanation

---

[1] *The Astral Plane*, p. 23. It is by the help of this magnifying power that the data presented by Dr. Besant and C. W. Leadbeater in *Occult Chemistry* is believed to have been obtained. Mr. Hodson, also, gives some experimental data on the atom, electron, radio-activity, etc., in his chapter " Clairvoyance," in *The Science of Seership*. In one place he says : " Focusing his [the writer's] consciousness within the atom, he experiences a sensation similar to that of gazing outwards into the solar system from a planet, and is struck with the similarity of construction and the relativity of magnitude ; he finds that the change of consciousness, resulting from the very high magnification, produces the illusion that, when the atom is examined in this way from a point within it, it is as immeasurably large as is a solar system." Mr. Hodson tells me, in fact, that he once almost lost himself in the " immensity " of an atom.

[2] A name given to the organs of our etheric and astral bodies, corresponding to the nerve-centres of our physical. See Frontispiece and Chapter X, " The Psychic Sense Organs," in Hodson's *The Science of Seership*, where this faculty of magnification is discussed.

performs the magnification is not clear. Four-dimensionally it is easily understandable. Compress the compass of your higher-space consciousness within suitable limits, and the object under examination looms up in inverse proportion.[1]

Reversibility

Lines 70–74 introduce us to another very interesting phenomenon, often referred to by occult investigators. The reader will remember that the number 13 was inscribed on the farther face of the cube, away from Mr. Hodson, but facing me, in the manner depicted in Fig. 1. When Mr. Hodson caught sight of the inscription clairvoyantly, he described the " 3 " as being on his right, and " normal " in position.

Now if the reader will place the page on which Fig. 1 is reproduced up against the light, examining the diagram from the rear (thus putting himself in the same position, relatively, that Mr. Hodson occupied), he will notice that the " 3 " is on the *left*, and instead of being in its " normal " position, it is " reversed." Had Mr. Hodson been using etheric vision, he would undoubtedly have seen the number 13[2] just

[1] The reader will find it interesting to compare this explanation with the slightly different one previously given in my *Theosophy and the Fourth Dimension*, p. 61.

[2] This was later verified experimentally. See lines 162–174.

as the reader sees it when looking through the rear of the paper (since, as we have said above, etheric vision is only a form of X-ray vision and nothing more). With true four-dimensional (*i.e.* astral) sight, however, the case is far different, as has already been indicated in Fig. 3 (*b*). We saw here that raising the visual power one dimension higher than the object looked at, enables one to see all sides at once, the words " front " and " back," " right " and " left " losing all definite meaning. Four-dimensional vision in this way possesses the peculiar faculty of entirely encompassing a physical object from all sides, so that every face appears to be in front of one. The number 13 would thus naturally be seen with astral vision as if the face on which it was inscribed were turned around facing the observer, and thus the " 3 " would be on the *right*, and in its " normal " position, just as Mr. Hodson reported.

The fact that this phenomenon of reversibility[1] is so easily explained four-dimensionally, and the many indications that I have had pointing to the fact that astral vision is

[1] This puzzling phenomenon of reversibility is alluded to by Dr. Besant in *The Ancient Wisdom*, p. 58, and by C. W. Leadbeater in *The Astral Plane*, pp. 12 and 19, and is explained from the mathematical standpoint in my *Theosophy and the Fourth Dimension*, pp. 58–59, to which the reader is referred, for a more detailed discussion.

four-dimensional in character, convince me that Mr. Hodson was at the time using clear four-dimensional (and therefore astral) vision, rather than etheric.[1]

As it happened, the conditions were reversed in the second experiment, both as regards the inscription's real position and Mr. Hodson's perception of it. The inscription faced away from him, as before, and appeared to me as in Fig. 2, upside down. Now if the reader will again turn the diagram to the light, looking through at it from the rear, he will see that the "3" is on the right, and reversed (just as Mr. Hodson reported it; see line 164), clearly indicating, therefore, that he was here using purely etheric, three-dimensional vision.[2]

---

[1] It is to be clearly understood that no part of this experiment was designed to prove the reality of clairvoyance or test Mr. Hodson's possession of the faculty. Such test experiments have already been performed and a reference to them will be found in Chapter II, "Clairvoyance as an instrument of scientific research," in Hodson's *The Science of Seership*. The present experiments were purely descriptive rather than evidential, and the analysis here presented therefore is offered to those who already know of the existence of such a faculty and have reasonable assurance that Mr. Hodson is possessed of it in some degree.

[2] This experiment, in my opinion, is a good deal more "evidential" than the former one, for the reason that the inscription had assumed the position shown in Fig. 2 after a good deal of twisting about, Mr. Hodson's eyes being closed the while. Even had Mr. Hodson known that it was upside-down, facing me, it would have taken an

It was possible, however, Mr. Hodson found, to go from etheric vision to astral, with a corresponding change in the manner in which the inscription was perceived. Thus, the " 13 " in Fig. 2 could also be seen, if desired, in its normal position, right-side up (indicating astral vision, see above). This, however, required a great effort of will this time, and something seemed to be constantly pulling him back to the lower order of vision, as if by a kind of natural elasticity, resisting the abnormal four-dimensional tension. Thus, for instance, would a bird feel, caught under a net and trying to rise into a freer dimension against the dead weight of the net itself.

The Four-Dimensional Counterpart of a Cube

Lines 33–65 constitute the most important feature of this series of experiments; they comprise, in fact, a description of the four-dimensional counterpart of a physical cube. Mr. Hodson here speaks of " diagonal extensions of all edges from the centre of the cube ; " then a sudden change : his mind jumps to the

---

immense effort of the imagination to determine whether the " 3 " seen *through* a transparent cube on the far side, should appear " normal " or " reversed." (The reader can test the truth of this statement for himself.) As a matter of fact, Mr. Hodson gave the information desired with practically no hesitation.

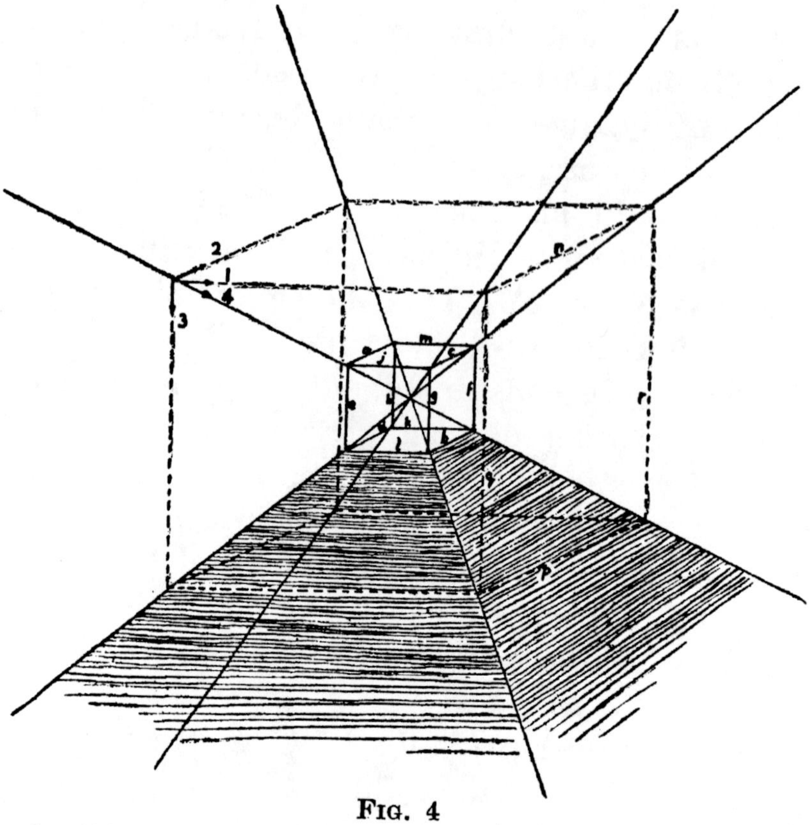

FIG. 4

An attempt to depict the superphysical counterpart of a cubical block, as seen by clairvoyant vision. The cube shown in dotted lines does not belong to the figure as reported by Mr. Hodson, and is merely included to facilitate its comprehension.

Notice how a three-dimensional cube has to be distorted when drawn on a two-dimensional surface. A four-dimensional figure such as the above necessarily suffers from a double dose of distortion.

The addition of the dotted lines brings out the close correspondence between the clairvoyant results and the Fig. 19 on p. 84 of *Theosophy and the Fourth Dimension.*

centre of the figure which now appears to him like a " spider's web in three dimensions," the edges having similar extension as before (suggesting the possibility that the two figures are really one, seen from two different points of view).

On the assumption that space is three-dimensional and Euclidean purely, it is difficult to conceive what possible significance can be attached to Mr. Hodson's description as here given. On the theory, however, that extension is possible in more than three dimensions, this description is full of significance.

Fig. 4 is a rough approximation of the object as it appeared to Mr. Hodson's clairvoyant vision. It is an attempt to portray a four-dimensional figure on a two-dimensional sheet of paper, and necessarily suffers from a double degree of distortion. Bearing this in mind, we can now proceed to analyse this somewhat formidable figure, preferably in conjunction with Fig. 19 and context, in *Theosophy and the Fourth Dimension,* which makes Fig. 4 very much more understandable.

We notice first a series of extensions from each of the twelve edges of the cube. Each of these extensions has the appearance of a two-dimensional sheet of light, radiating off at apparently a forty-five degree angle.[1]

[1] I say " apparently " because subsequent investigation showed that this radiation was in another dimension entirely, and actually at right angles to all three edges of the physical cube. This, by definition, constitutes the " fourth dimension." In depicting this fourth dimension on two-dimensional paper, we are forced to distort it, just as we do when depicting the third dimension.

The reader should at this point go around the cube mentally, counting off the twelve sheets of light, the better to fix the figure in his mind. He will notice that the physical cube is bounded by the twelve edges *a*, *b*, *c*, etc., and that from each of these edges a sheet of light seems to spread out, twelve in all.

The figure can be visualized in another way as well. Taking each square face of the cube, a truncated pyramid can be seen to radiate out : downwards from *dkbl*, towards the right from *gcfb*, etc. There are six such truncated pyramids. The bases of each of these pyramids can be seen in the six faces of the dotted cube. These truncated pyramids are clearly shown in Fig. 21, p. 88, of *Theosophy and the Fourth Dimension*. In Fig. 4, the truncated pyramids do not of course stop at the mathematical boundary lines shown in dotted form, but continue to radiate out beyond these artificial limitations, apparently, since Mr. Hodson reported no such limitations as are here drawn.

We now notice that the radiating sheets, in addition to spreading outwards, also penetrate inwards, all twelve radiating planes apparently meeting in a point at the centre of the cube.[1] The truncated pyramids we have before noticed now become perfect pyramids, having one common apex.

---

[1] Cf. lines 35, 36 above.

If we now take the two radiating sheets *a* and *b*, we notice that they are actually seen to be in the same plane. The same applies to the opposite two radiating sheets, *c* and *d*, as depicted more clearly in Fig. 5. Here we see the figure X that Mr. Hodson speaks of in lines 49–52.

But we soon find that we can perform the same operation mentally with the radiations *jk* and *ml*, thus forming a figure X at right angles to the first. A third figure X is still possible if we take the pair of radiations *ef* and *gh*, and this we find is at right angles to the two former X figures. If now we find Mr. Hodson saying[1] that vision is "rendered difficult at this point by sudden appearance of cross-sections at different angles," we can heartily sympathize with him, the more so when we try to visualize what this triple-X figure must look like when pictured as an intersecting whole. It is as if a two-dimensional microbe were to find himself at the centre of an exploding shell, trying to follow at one and the same time the motion of the shattered particles in every direction. Our microbe, if he became articulate, might similarly describe the exploding shell as a "pulsing, living, entity, a kind of engine" (lines 54–55), and might further be moved to speak as Mr. Hodson does in lines 69–65.

---

[1] Lines 55–57.

It by this time takes no very strong effort of the imagination to picture the plane *ab* as an uncompleted portion of a spider's web; *cd* is another such partial web. Each of the other

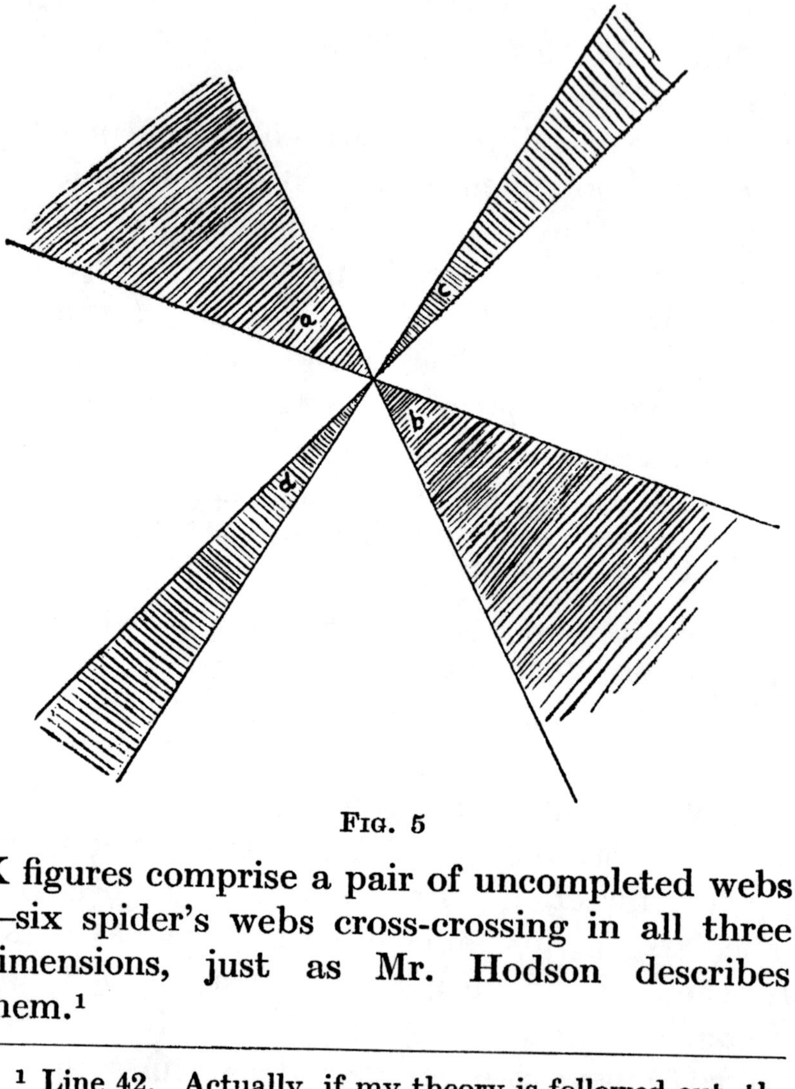

FIG. 5

X figures comprise a pair of uncompleted webs —six spider's webs cross-crossing in all three dimensions, just as Mr. Hodson describes them.[1]

[1] Line 42. Actually, if my theory is followed out, the compound spider's web would be in four dimensions, and not in three only, but even four-dimensional figures are

Now if Fig. 4 correctly depicts what Mr. Hodson has seen (as far as any two-dimensional diagram can depict a figure of more than two dimensions), its resemblance to Fig. 19[1] is apparent. In the latter figure, *abcdefgh* represents a physical cube such as the one Mr. Hodson was examining. The radiations extending from each of the edges here terminate in an outer cube *ABCDEFGH*. This extension encloses an ideal four-dimensional figure, the tesseract. In the case of Fig. 4, however, the radiations continue on, as we have seen. Despite this difference between the two figures, the tesseract of Fig. 19 can easily be seen to constitute the basic element of the figure depicted in Fig. 4, just as the square is the basic element of every solid object.

There is another and more serious difference between the two figures, however, and this requires some elucidation. In Fig. 4 we find that the radiating planes, instead of having their source at the edges of the physical cube, as they do in Fig. 19, actually seem to go inwards, terminating apparently in a point, the apex of the six pyramids previously referred to. What must actually happen is suggested in Fig. 22.[2]

---

normally seen three-dimensionally, due to a peculiar tendency of the human mind. See under "Negative results," below.

[1] *Op. cit.*, p. 84. [2] *Op. cit.*, p. 89.

Here *K–L* represents the physical cube, and the radiating planes, beginning at the edges, go inwards as well as outwards, and terminate in the inward direction in the cube *a–g*. Were we to continue the radiation inward, however, the cube would appear to shrink still further, and would finally terminate in a mathematical point, having its location to all appearances in the centre of the cube, as shown in Fig. 4.

Now on the assumption that what Mr. Hodson saw was a true four-dimensional figure (and we will ask the reader to allow this assumption for the time being, till it is definitely established), then the radiating planes in Fig. 4 are in true four-dimensional space, just as they are in Figs. 19 and 22.[1] The line *a–A*, for instance (Figs. 19 and 22), is a true fourth dimension, at right angles to each of the three physical dimensions of the cube; and the entire plane *ehEH* shoots off into the fourth dimension, at right angles to all the faces of the cube. Similarly with all the other radiating planes.

However, if each of the lines *Aa, Ee, Hh, Dd,* are at right angles to the plane *AEHD,* then it is evident that what appears to be a truncated pyramid, having its base in *AEHD,* is only a vastly distorted picture of a true cube (just as the photograph of a skyscraper taken from the

[1] The reader will find a study of pp. 80–91, *op. cit.*, to be a decided advantage in the comprehension of the entire subject of four-dimensional vision, as here treated.

street appears distorted). Hence the square *aehd* is equal in size to *AEHD*, appearing smaller only on account of four-dimensional perspective. In Fig. 22 the same argument holds true. The entire cube *a–g*, in fact, is but a replica of the physical cube *K–L*, the apparent shrinkage being an optical illusion.

We now have no difficulty in seeing that what appears to be a series of pyramids meeting in a common apex is only a series of cubes, apparently converging " inwards " into four-dimensional space, giving the appearance of a cube shrinking to a point in far-off higher (or inner) space. This end-cube, which looks like a point in the distance, is not really in the centre of the physical cube at all. It is in a different order of space entirely. Motion " inwards " and " outwards " is at all times a parallel motion, just as progression along a pair of tracks is at all times a parallel motion.

If all these speculations are well-founded, it seemed to me that it should be possible to actually *experience* this parallel motion, this motion-without-convergence. During the course of the second experiment I accordingly asked Mr. Hodson to concentrate his vision on one of the points of the physical cube, and then follow this point " inwards," towards what he called " the centre of the cube." What Mr. Hodson saw upon doing so, greatly surprised him. The line of progression, in the first place, seemed to recede without actually appearing

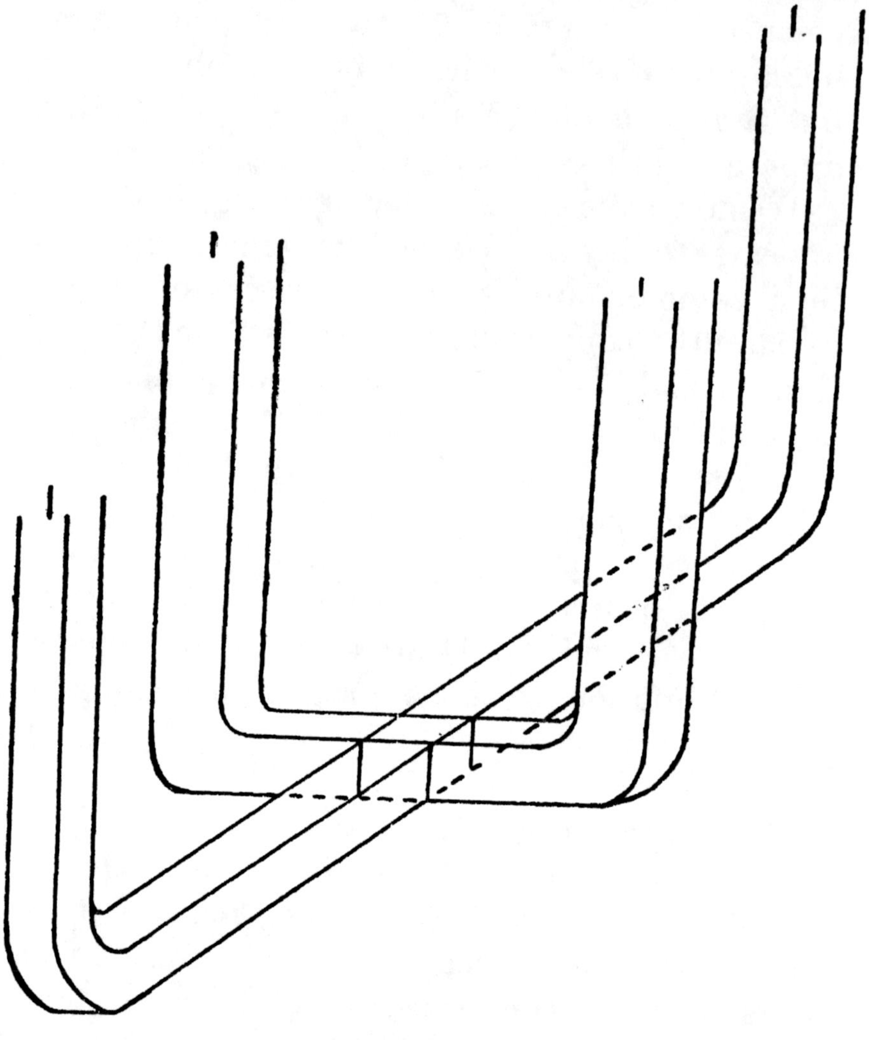

FIG. 6

to leave its position (incomprehensible to him at the time, but perfectly clear from a four-dimensional standpoint); it no longer moved "inside" the physical cube, but "inwards" in a mysterious sense. Furthermore, the progression now appeared to him as a true parallel motion, free of the illusion of perspec-

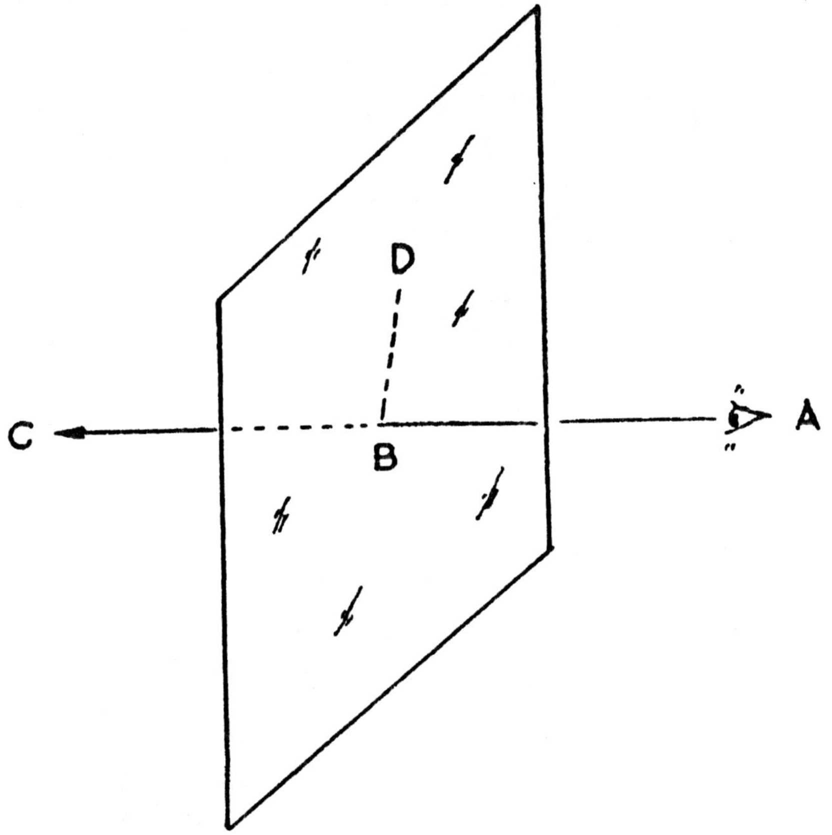

FIG. 8

tive. As far as he could go, the cubes now appeared to be all of equal size, nowhere really coming to a point, as he had at first thought. This once more established the experiment in my own mind as being of a four-dimensional order, since four-dimensional theory made absolutely clear a phenomenon which to three-dimensional thought is entirely incomprehensible.[1]

Further Descriptions

In lines 75–78 Mr. Hodson speaks of a " U " being seen, having the appearance of a rectangular block-letter passing through the physical cube at its bottom. Then he speaks

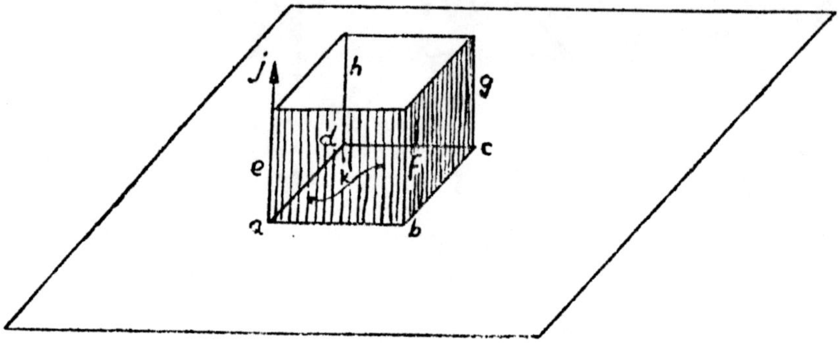

Fig. 9

of two " U's," their intersection making the physical cube, as indicated in Fig. 6.

In lines 43–46 Mr. Hodson speaks of an extension of each of the sides, as shown in Fig. 7; this is referred to again in line 94. Striving to determine the significance of these " U " and cross-forms, Mr. Hodson was of the opinion that "the cross and the 'U' are cross-sections of the causal (or archetypal) cube," and have no real objective existence in

[1] This phenomenon is discussed in greater detail under Remarks on the Second Experiment, below.

themselves, being rather of the nature of mental perceptions than objective realities. He was convinced, on the other hand, that the edge-extended figure as depicted in Fig. 4, had definite objective reality, independent of the observer's mind. (See Third Experiment, lines 236–296.)

Neither the "U" nor the cross-form, as far as I can see at present, are capable of analysis on a four-dimensional basis, and I therefore leave the record without further comment.

REMARKS ON THE SECOND EXPERIMENT

THE major portion of this experiment has already been discussed in conjunction with what has gone before. The following additional remarks may be of interest :

Lines 127–132. It is clear that Mr. Hodson only describes one of the two directions in which motion takes place, the omission of the second direction not being noticed at the time. We can, however, supply the missing information from the results of the First Experiment : one motion is an expansion outwards ; the other, a contraction inwards. Both " expansion " and " contraction " are of course optical illusions, produced by visual distortion, as has already been explained ; both " outwards " and " inwards " are directions in the fourth dimension—just as " up " and " down " in Fig. 3 are directions in the third dimension.

Lines 141–161 *and* 175–200. This also has been partially touched upon already. The apparent paradox of a point moving and yet not moving (line 154) is easily explained by an analogy (see Figs. 8 and 9).

Imagine a person at *A* (Fig. 8) looking at a point *B* on a window-pane. Any motion of the point along the plane (as, for instance, towards the point *D*) will be clearly noticeable. But

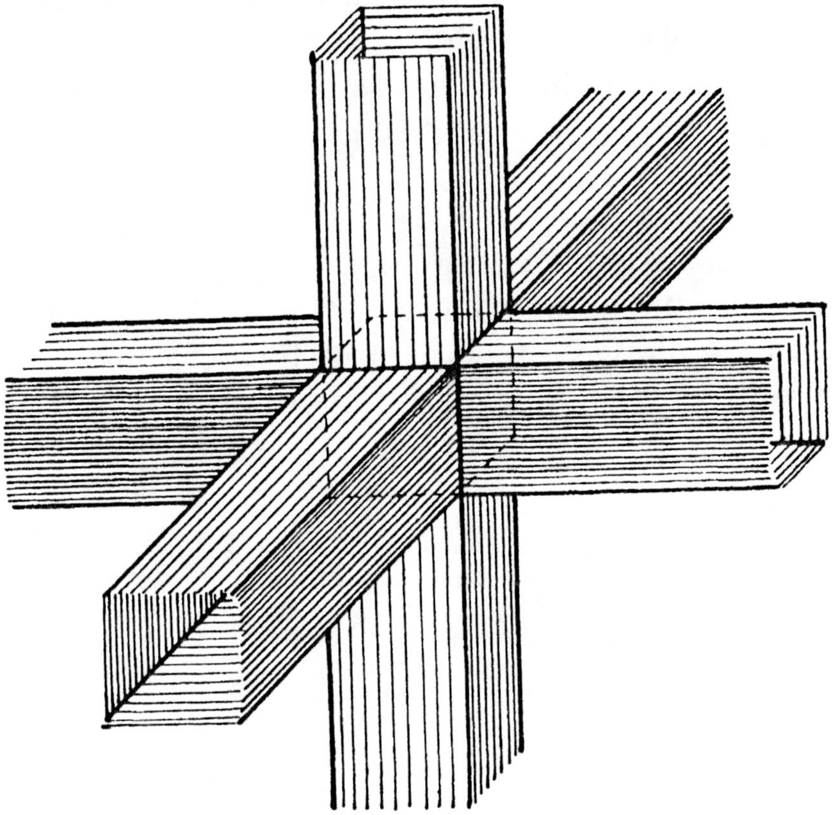

FIG. 7

any motion along the line of sight perpendicular to the plane (towards the point *C*) can never be discerned; *C* and *B* would appear to occupy the same space.

A two-dimensional microbe, examining a physical cube clairvoyantly, would have the same experience. In attempting to follow out the progression of the base-square *abcd* in the direction of the third dimension, it would find that at each corner, motion would take place in such a manner that the motion itself is indiscernible. Thus, at the point *a*, motion in the direction *aj* would be along the direct line of sight, and the progression from *a* to *j* could very fittingly be described as " motion without motion."

Going a step further, we find the same motion-without-motion in Mr. Hodson's case as well, indicating that Mr. Hodson was at the time looking directly into four-dimensional space, at right angles to physical space.

REMARKS ON THE THIRD EXPERIMENT

THE purport of the first question put to Mr. Hodson (which has an important bearing on our understanding of the constitution of four-dimensional substance) can be best appreciated by having recourse again to our two-dimensional analogy, with our hypothetical microbe performing a clairvoyant examination of a square *abcd*, as in Fig. 9.

This square, the reader will remember, is a physical reality to a two-dimensional being, and in describing its " astral " counterpart (which, to us, is a physical cube), he would say that he sees, at each of the four corners, a radiation " inwards " or " upwards," *e*, *f*, *g*, *h*. However, this in itself does not constitute a solid cube, since the space enclosed by the radiations is apparently empty. It is so far no more than an inverted bridge-table.

Upon closer examination, however, our clairvoyant observer finds that this radiation extends, not only from the four corners, but from every point along the edge of the square, the summation of these vertical lines forming a plane surface as at *k*. Similar radiations from each of the other sides of the square would give us the form of a hollow box instead of, as before, an inverted bridge-table.

Virtually the same condition obtains in

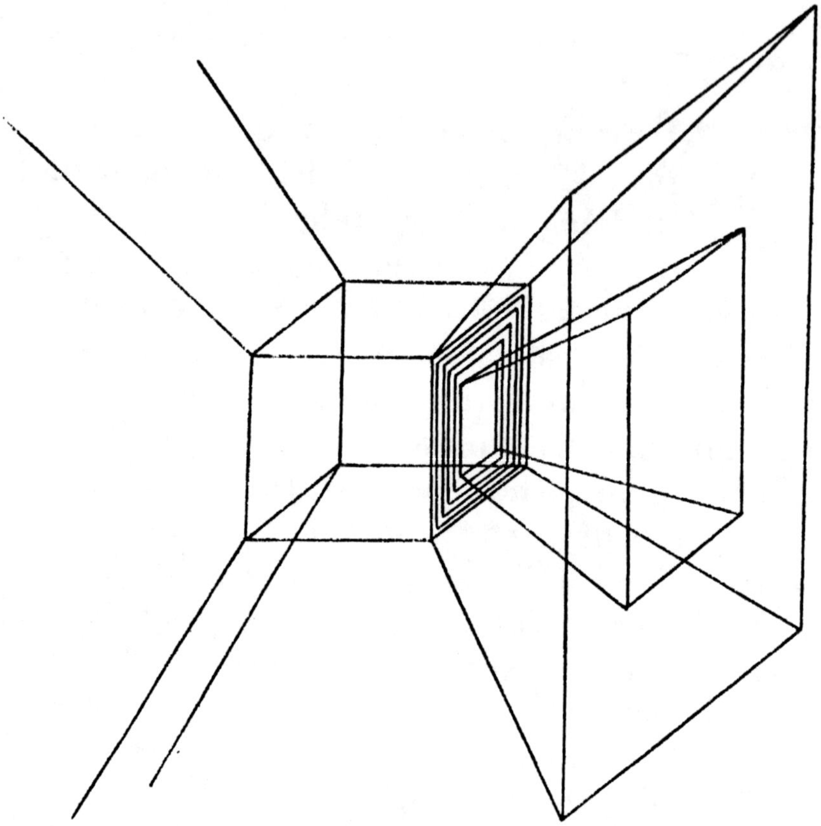

Fig. 10

Fig. 10, which partly illustrates in diagrammatic form the physical cube as observed by Mr. Hodson. Here we notice that everything has been " stepped up " one dimension. We find our edge-extended figure as before, but Mr. Hodson now notices that if he directs his gaze at the surface of one of the sides, there is a curious pyramidical extension not only from the edges of the square, but from each one of the infinite series of squares that can be drawn inside that outer square. (One of these additional pyramidical extensions is shown in the diagram.) Therc is thus, not only a radiation from the edges, but from the entire face of the cube, forming a solid, three-dimensional figure extending from the physical cube into four-space. The reader will hardly have to be reminded now that this pyramidical form is really a cubical form in perspective.

Similar cubes, of course, extend from each of the six faces of our physical base-cube, and these may be thought of as " surrounding " our four-dimensional figure—the " astral " counterpart of the cube—just as the four radiating planes in Fig. 9 surround the three-dimensional figure there shown.

So far, we have, in Figs. 10 and 4, what we might call a hollow four-dimensional box, bounded, not by planes (as three-dimensional boxes are) but by cubes. Fig. 4, then, is not a perfect tesseract, but may be called a tesseractoid, just as Fig. 9 is not a cube, but a cuboid. In order to make this latter figure an actual " solid " in the true sense, a still further filling-in has to be carried out in the three-dimensional space enclosed by the radiating planes. Similarly, in order to make Fig. 4 a true tesseract, a like filling-in would have to exist in the four-dimensional space enclosed by the cubical extensions which surround it. Whether or not this space is actually so filled in, was not investigated in these experiments, and further research should be conducted to elucidate this point.

The answer to question 4 (lines 297–304, referring to line 39 in the first experiment), however, would seem to suggest that the four-dimensional space we are discussing is in reality "filled in" in the manner required by the theory, thus giving us a figure having all the characteristics of four-directional solidity. Much more definite investigation, however, will have to be carried out before this question can be truthfully said to be settled.

REMARKS ON THE FOURTH EXPERIMENT

THE first question asked was unfortunately based upon a misconception on my part, hence the discrepancies in the reply. This misconception soon became apparent, and the question was consequently not pursued any further.[1]

At the point indicated by the second question, a closed book (free of inscription on the cover) was placed before Mr. Hodson, in such a way that he had no way of determining the position of the text within. In the answer to this question, only lines 344–345 have mathematical significance; the remainder of the answer will therefore not be commented upon here. The purpose of the question itself was merely to pave the way for question 3.

The reader is asked to note the phrase, "the text of the book is seen as an interlocking fretwork." A sheet, printed on both sides, and held up to the light, would be found to have a

[1] I think it speaks well for the genuineness of Mr. Hodson's clairvoyant faculties that he did not fall in with the trend of the question and give the kind of answer that the form of the question itself called for.

similar appearance of fretwork design, due to the interlocking effect of the print on the reverse side of the sheet. This indicates a fact that we have previously noted, namely, that etheric vision is merely a kind of X-ray sight, that is, merely an extension of physical, three-dimensional vision, no mathematical change taking place in the space characteristics of the observer's consciousness.

With astral vision, however, the case is far different, as we again have already had occasion to note. In the present case, the text was correctly seen as being upside-down. What is of greater significance, however (from the mathematical standpoint), is that no "fret-work" or interlocking effect was noticed when astral vision was used, the effect being similar to the appearance of an open book, both pages being clearly seen in their right relation, the reverse pages being seen "normal" instead of "reversed." Here again we meet with the phenomenon of reversibility, possessed by astral vision, but not by etheric. This is just what the four-dimensional theory would call for, and once again we find evidence establishing the fact that astral vision is definitely four-dimensional in character.[1]

---

[1] The severely critical reader will possibly observe that in some instances I seem to be reasoning in a circle: I start out with certain assumptions with respect to etheric and astral vision, calling one three-dimensional and the

This is still further borne out by the answer to question 4. Hence we find that, in spite of the book being actually upside-down with respect to Mr. Hodson's position, it could be seen clairvoyantly as either upside-down or right-side up, at will, when astral vision was turned on, but not when etheric vision was used. This is another phase of reversibility, and is easily explainable in four-dimensional terms.[1]

It was with the view to establishing beyond possibility of doubt at least one fundamental difference between etheric and astral clairvoyance that I asked Mr. Hodson to see whether the phenomenon of reversibility was possible with etheric vision. Mr. Hodson tried again and again, but as the record shows, finally had to give it up as a bad job, almost

---

other four-dimensional, and then proceed to "prove" what I have in the first place assumed. From the standpoint of the present monograph, taken by itself, the criticism is fully justified, and I make no pretence of putting before the reader a closely reasoned, step-by-step exposition of four-dimensional theory and its clairvoyant corroboration. Such an exposition would take us beyond the purpose and limits of the present work. The subject is admittedly involved, and the field of investigation has only been roughly sketched in here. The careful student, however, will be able to fill in the desired steps in the reasoning process by making a study of the existing works on the Fourth Dimension and occult phenomena (see Bibliography, below).

[1] See *Theosophy and the Fourth Dimension*, pp. 45–50 and 58–60 for a detailed discussion of this interesting phenomenon.

apologetically, feeling no doubt that his clairvoyant power had for once failed him. The very opposite, however, is true, and I feel once again that this apparently inconsequent incident established Mr. Hodson's *bona fides* as an occult observer, since it was so easy to fall in with the apparent trend of my question and answer in the affirmative.

REMARKS ON THE FIFTH EXPERIMENT

A FEW preliminary observations are necessary in order to appreciate the object of this experiment.

Let me begin by saying that there are several points of view from which the theory of the Fourth Dimension can be discussed.

This arises from the fact that the designation "fourth" in the order of dimensions is purely arbitrary, there being in reality an infinite number of "fourth" dimensions possible.[1] One of these "fourth" dimensions appears, from the accounts given by occult observers, to lie in the direction of astral space. Another "fourth" dimension has been appropriated by the Relativists, and has been called Time. Physical reality, according to the latter school, is actually four-dimensional. Three of these dimensions are static, and are apprehended simultaneously; the fourth we apprehend only progressively, so to speak, and is for this reason called Time.

To make clear the relation that exists

[1] See *Theosophy and the Fourth Dimension*, pp. 34-36.

between these dimensions, let us take an analogy from the realm of railway transportation. In this analogy, we picture a two-dimensional surface: North-and-South being the first dimension, and East-and-West the second. Assuming the railway line to run in the latter dimension, we can picture it as being measured off by appropriate milestones and stations along the way.

It becomes at once apparent, however, that a traveller can only " know " these milestones or stations one at a time. Given a constant speed, these stations can just as conveniently be thought of in terms of time as of space. Thus, we say, two stations are an hour apart. The concept of time is here only a mechanism used to measure an extension which is in itself purely spatial. In like manner, astronomers find it more convenient to speak of enormous distances in terms of light-years.

Looked at from this point of view, Time becomes only a measure of space. Reality is four-dimensional, and as the plane of consciousness moves through it, we call the measure of this motion, Time. Since this motion is nowhere within the three-dimensional world, we say that it constitutes a totally new dimension, the Fourth.

Now, returning to our railway traveller, and assuming that he travels with constant speed in one direction only,[1] we find that he has a tendency to call the position he happens to occupy at any one moment "the present," while the space that he has already traversed is to him "the past" and that which he has yet to traverse is "the future." But these terms, we know, are true only for *his* consciousness; they are purely relative and have no objective basis in themselves. In reality, all the milestones and all the railway stations are in simultaneous existence; it is only the limitations under which he exists that impose upon him the concept of Time. Were he to take an airplane and rise into a higher dimension—the third—he would indeed see the entire line simultaneously; to him the terms past, present, and future, would then lose all significance. He would be able, to be sure, to look

---

[1] According to Dr. Robb, this uni-directional limitation constitutes the fundamental difference between space and time, for, whereas motion in space is under control as to speed, and reversible as to direction, motion in time is not. (W. R. C. Coode Adams, *A Primer of Occult Physics*, p. 10.) This motion, it must be remarked, presupposes the *simultaneous existence* of two points separated by the element "time." In fact, it is even doubtful in some minds whether it is any longer permissible to speak of "time" as separating any two points, since time to them does not seem to have any independent reality of its own. It is actually "space" that separates these two points, and "time" is only our relative yardstick for measuring that space—a mental gauge and no more. (For a continuation of this discussion, see Appendix.)

down on the progress of a certain train and enter into the spirit of a passenger's consciousness; he would be able to run his eye backwards and forwards and look into the passenger's "past" and "future." But to him—and this is the important point—this past as well as this future are both immediately present with a sense of an eternal "now" that is almost inconceivable to the limited consciousness of the passenger below.

"Step up" the above analogy one dimension, and we have a true picture of our physical life. Physical reality (without encroaching upon the space of the astral or any other world), as has been said, is viewed as being actually four-dimensional. The "plane" of consciousness, however, cuts a section through this reality, and since a section is at all times one dimension less than the thing sectioned, this section of consciousness becomes inevitably three-dimensional. Because our plane of consciousness is in continual motion, it cuts fresh sections continuously, and the change that takes place in our consciousness under the influence of this passing panorama, we call Time. The innumerable sections we have left behind us, constitute "the past"; the innumerable sections still to be cut, form "the future." All sections, however—past, present, and future—are in eternal existence now; the space separating events can just as conveniently be expressed in miles as in hours.[1] All sections taken together give us the entire reality.[2] "If we could see and know a thing in *all* its relations and proportions—the 'thing in itself'—it would disclose to us the whole universe, past, present, and future."[3]

Mr. Hodson's Experience

We are now, I hope, in a better position to appreciate to the full the value and importance of Mr. Hodson's experience in four-dimensional vision, as recorded in the Fifth Experiment.

The reader will notice that in lines 382–387, Mr. Hodson speaks of a progression from what we might term his "present" body to his

---

[1] Algebraically, the space separating two events can be expressed by the formula $S = Kh$ miles, where K is a constant representing the speed with which our plane of consciousness traverses four-dimensional space, and h is the distance between the events measured by time. The speed K we of course do not know, but assuming arbitrarily (for the sake of illustration) a speed of ten miles per year, a century would be a thousand miles long, and twenty thousand miles would be the distance we would have to travel (in round numbers) to bring before our eyes the scenes of Julius Cæsar's Rome.

[2] Imagine a strip of motion-picture film, depicting the historical growth of a city, cut up into individual "frames," and arranged so that one frame is superimposed upon another, in chronological order. Here, the dimensions of space are compressed into two, and the third dimension represents "time." In this analogy, the space between two events is actually measurable in inches.

[3] W. Kingsland, *The Physics of the Secret Doctrine*, p. 47.

"baby" body, which motion he feels (very rightly) to be similar in character to the inward motion of the cube in the previous experiments. This suggests its four-dimensional character and furnishes us with a basis for comparison with the geometrical facts we have already adduced in connection with three and four-dimensional space-relations.

In this progression "inwards," he sees a physical body wherever his mind happens to stop—"apparently inside" (line 401), just as the inner cubes appeared to be "inside" the physical cube he was examining. And just as these inner cubes were actual realities, and not merely mental representations, *so is each of these bodies an actual physical reality to Mr. Hodson's supernormal vision.* This point is important; in fact, it is the crux of the whole situation, and will be referred to again.

As for the bodies being "inside" him, it will of course be understood by now just in what sense they are spoken of as "inside"; Mr. Hodson, as a matter of fact, felt all the while that this sense of "inside" was only an illusion. "Within" would of course be a better word, the direction itself being four-dimensional. In a like manner, just as the "past" was within, so did the "future" seem to be "without"—an external continuation, apparently, of his "present" body "outwards." (In the case of the cube, the reader will remember that there was a similar extension " outwards " in the direction of the fourth dimension.) The extension in the present case did not make the " future " body appear to be any bigger than the present one (lines 430–431), thus again confirming the extension as being of a parallel character in the direction of the fourth dimension.

Thus is the physical body seen as a four-dimensional object, of which the " present " is only a three-dimensional cross-section. A portion of this four-dimensional super-body stretches out into one direction in four-space and we call it " the past," merely because it has already projected itself upon the plane of consciousness. Another portion of this super-body stretches out into another direction in four-space and we call it " the future " for an equally arbitrary reason ; namely, because it has not yet projected itself in this manner. But these projections are mere shadows cast on the wall of consciousness, very much like the shadows in Plato's famous allegory. The Reality—that which is casting the shadows—is a four-dimensional synthesis of past, present, and future in one indivisible unity.[1]

---

[1] " The real person," said H. P. Blavatsky, " . . . is composed of the sum of all its various and changing conditions from its appearance in material form to its disappearance from earth . . . which, dropping out of the ' to be ' into the ' has been,' out of the future into the past

In lines 415–425 Mr. Hodson actually experiences this four-dimensional reality—not to be confused with his Ego, or even his astral body—but merely his physical body extending in four directions. The time-limitations that are so characteristic of our normal life are here transcended; the reality is seen to be not only the "present" body but actually a summation of all states of that body from end to end of life. The real personality is not merely the temporary, evanescent cross-section manifested at any one period of life, but the summation of all the cross-sections that are traversed from birth to death, conceived as a synthetic whole. In a similar manner is the reality of a railway line represented by a summation of the infinite points that extend from one end to the other. A summation of planes likewise gives us a solid; a summation of solids gives us a tesseractoid.[1]

—present momentarily to our senses a cross-section, as it were, of their total selves, as they pass through time and space (as matter) on their way from one eternity to another: and these two eternities constitute that Duration in which alone anything has true existence, were our senses but able to cognize it." *The Secret Doctrine*, vol. 1, 3rd ed., p. 69.

See pp. 27–36 and 71–72 in *Theosophy and the Fourth Dimension* for a more detailed discussion of time as a fourth dimension.

[1] Moralists will no doubt see here a valuable analogy (though somewhat beside the present subject): a man must not be judged by his character and actions at any

The Present Reality of " Past " Events

It was strongly brought out during the experiment (lines 454–469) that the " past " possessed a physical reality that was far different from a mere " memory." This was thoroughly discussed at the time of the experiment, as the record shows, and the fact emphasized that, as far as Mr. Hodson's consciousness went, he felt he was looking at a physical reality actually present before his gaze, having all the solidity of a physical object. It was definitely not a case of looking back in imagination over his mental storehouse of memories, nor was it an objective projection of his imagination; it was not even looking at the " astral light " or the " akashic records " or the " memory of nature," as it has been variously called. It was very definitely not something which merely " had been " but was no longer in objective existence now. Quite the contrary, he had the feeling all the time that he was gazing at a solid, objective, physical reality. This point cannot be overemphasized, however tedious it may become,

---

one moment—one must enter into the spirit of his entire past and know the forces, innate and environmental, that have led him to be what he is; one must likewise see the destiny that lies ahead of him, his mission and function in life, so to speak, before a correct appraisal may be reached. For his real nature exists much more in the " past " and " future " than in the " present."

for, as intimated above, it forms the crux of the whole experiment.

THE RATIONALE OF PSYCHOMETRY

The bearing that the above has on the question of psychometry is at once apparent. For the benefit of those to whom the subject is somewhat unfamiliar, I might say that the faculty of psychometry—one of whose characteristics is the ability to " see " past events —is ordinarily explained by saying that

> every object is surrounded by, and exists in, a sea of *Akash,* upon which is indelibly imprinted a record of its complete history. . . .[1]

Contact with an object psychometrized produces in the mind of the clairvoyant a vision of its past history, and the psychometrist becomes apparently able to focus his attention on any part of that history at will. It is interesting to note, however, that Mr. Hodson, both in the present experiment and in the book referred to, does not seem quite satisfied with the " akashic record " theory, and he asks the pertinent question :

> By what mechanism is the stored-up vibration translated into vivid pictures within the mind's eye or inner consciousness of the seer ? In other words, how does a vibratory power, surrounding and penetrating an object, become a picture ?

---

[1] Chapter on " Psychometry " in Hodson's *The Science of Seership.*

> Further, by what mechanism is the seer enabled, not only to observe the picture as a spectator, but to enter into it, and to place his consciousness at the actual place of occurrence? The second change is, if possible, more remarkable than the first, for the seer changes from an observer of a more or less small picture to a participator in the actual scene; whereupon the picture is no longer an external concentration of an event before his mind's eye, but becomes a complete environment.[1]

A still further difficulty arises from the fact that it is not only the past that can be seen, but the future also. Here the "akashic record" theory falls down completely, at least in the terms in which it is at present couched in occult literature, and we find we must have recourse to a different conception entirely if we are ever to understand this phenomenon. Mr. Hodson correctly suggests that the explanation of that latter phenomenon lies in "the relativity of time and the elusive conception of the eternal NOW."[1] But as soon as we do this, we embark on the sea of four-dimensional reasoning.

A very clear picture of the physical *reality* of the things seen is brought home to us in the description Mr. Hodson gives of this phenomenon.

> Apparently neither time nor space have any power to limit the range of the psychometrist's powers. Hand him an object from the ruins of the

---

[1] *Loc. cit.*

temple of St. Colomb on Iona, and he does not see Iona as viewed from his present position in time and space; he sees it as it actually was at any period of its history he may desire, *as if he himself were present in that period.*[1] He does not view it as through a telescope from his study, but stands upon the island, and within the temple if he wishes. He hears the waves beating on the shores of the island; he feels the climatic conditions, and may actually endure extremes of cold or heat in his present physical body. Whether the object is ten thousand years or only one year old, its history is visible to the psychometrist's inner eye.

The reader will by now have noticed how much more intelligible the above phenomenon becomes in the light of the four-dimensional theory and how the questions that Mr. Hodson raises tend to answer themselves. A study of the entire chapter on Psychometry from which the above quotations have been taken will now prove very profitable.

In this connection, it is interesting to read, in a still (at this writing) unpublished MS. of Mr. Hodson's, a message dictated to him on April 26, 1929, part of which reads as follows:

Everything is Absolute and Infinite. . . .

From this level of consciousness, even the theory of evolution is a fallacy, for everything *is* all at once, in all its fullness. Nothing "becomes" anything else. The virginal does not "become" productive; good does not "become" evil; the happy does not "become" the miserable; all these things *are* at the same time. They are implicit in the one fact

[1] Mr. Hodson's italics.

—the One Existence—the One Life. If we realize this, we have all.

The question, " Why does the Infinite become the Finite ? " is based upon a false premise ; it does not. The idea of " become " is the error ; it must be replaced by " is."

PART III

SUMMARY OF RESULTS OBTAINED

IT would perhaps be well to summarize the facts that now seem to be at least provisionally established by the preceding experiments, realizing of course that these experiments cannot be taken by themselves, but only as forming part of a continuous whole, reaching out into the wider domain of occult research. The following represent some of these results :

1. Clairvoyance-in-space is four-dimensional in character ; that is, its rationale can be conveniently explained in terms of the four-dimensional theory. This form of clairvoyance, in other words, consists in focussing the consciousness at a point in four-dimensional space, and looking down, so to speak, on to the physical plane from that eminence. Raising the consciousness to a point in some organ of the astral body would satisfy this condition, since the astral body is believed to be four-dimensional.[1]

---

[1] This follows from the fact that astral phenomena can be interpreted and explained four-dimensionally. This, however, could well form the subject of further research. See Suggestions, 2, below.

2. Four-dimensional vision results in the following phenomena :

(*a*) Transparency of solid matter (2, 66–69, 133, 162–174, 355–373).[1]

(*b*) Ability to see all around a solid object at once (15, 70–74).

(*c*) Reversibility (70–74, 166–173, 358–365).

- (*a*) transcends such notions as " inside " " outside," since one is as clearly visible as the other ;
- (*b*) transcends such notions as " front," " back," " top," " bottom " ;
- (*c*) transcends such notions as " right," " left," " upside-down," " down-side up," since all these are purely three-dimensional limitations and have no meaning in four-dimensional vision.

(*d*) Magnification (10, 24–29, 139).

(*e*) Isometric vision ; that is, freedom from the illusions of perspective (11–13).

3. The physical cube examined is in reality a four-dimensional object (Fig. 4). This four-dimensional object is bounded by three-dimensional solids, as required by the theory (206–221).

While it is hazardous to generalize from an examination of a single object, the fact that this examination (repeated on several occasions) corroborates in so many ways the

---

[1] These numbers refer to the lines in the Record of Experiments.

four-dimensional theory, makes it safe to say that three-dimensional physical objects, generally, are in reality four-dimensional.[1]

4. The physical cube (and therefore probably every physical object) is not static but dynamic, the flow of energy being clearly visible as extending into four-dimensional space (54, 64, 103, 128, 232–235, 242–252).

5. The distinction between etheric and astral vision can be expressed mathematically; one is three-dimensional, the other is four-dimensional.

Etheric vision also confers transparency, but without reversibility (369–373).

6. Time as a fourth dimension appears to be a physical reality, and not merely an intellectual or scientific fiction. The human body, for instance, is four-dimensional. Past, present, and future, are merely human designations; it is possible for a human being to free himself from three-dimensional limitations, and in this condition the entire four-dimensional reality can be viewed.

7. Psychometry is more easily explained as a vision of this four-dimensional reality, than on the assumption that physical events register themselves on a sensitive medium, the *akasha*.

---

[1] See below, Suggestions, 3.

NEGATIVE RESULTS

A WORD may now be said on the subject of the apparently negative results obtained in two instances.

1. Mr. Hodson, contrary to my expectations, did not see a tesseract. That is, upon applying four-dimensional vision, he did not at once become conscious of four-directional extension, as the theory would suppose. Even when gazing at what is very evidently a tesseractoid (Fig. 4), he did not clearly perceive that it had four dimensions; he saw it, in other words, three-dimensionally. The human mind seems to have a bent for seeing three-dimensionally, and it appears that even four-dimensional objects have a tendency to be retranslated in consciousness in terms of three.

A similar failure on the part of other clairvoyant investigators to clearly describe astral figures four-dimensionally has often puzzled me in the past. Assuming that astral bodies are in reality four-dimensional (a fairly safe assumption, seeing in how many different ways four-dimensional theory clarifies and corroborates astral observations),[1] it would seem at first sight that no difficulty should be experienced in seeing the four dimensions clearly, each one at right angles to the other three. Such, however, is not generally the case, though C. W. Leadbeater does say: "I can at any rate bear witness that the tesseract, or four-dimensional cube, is a reality, for it is quite a familiar figure on the astral plane."[2]

The difficulty mentioned above has some analogies in ordinary consciousness. Thus, we are familiar with the fact that the photographic plate reduces three-dimensional objects to two-dimensional terms. We, who are thoroughly accustomed to the notion of perspective, retranslate this two-dimensional picture into three dimensions. It is said, however, that some aborigines are unable to do that, and to them a photograph is consequently blank and meaningless. Children, again, are said to have an analogous difficulty during early infancy, their inability to judge distance being due to their lack—or insufficient development—of the sense of perspective. It appears that they begin by seeing two-dimensionally. According to Ouspensky, animals similarly see only two-dimensionally, though this view involves very evident difficulties.

---

1 See *Theosophy and the Fourth Dimension*, chapter "The Astral Plane."

2 Claude Bragdon, *A Primer of Higher Space*, p. 30.

It is interesting to note, however, one mitigating fact in this "negative result," and that is, that Mr Hodson did succeed in giving a clear description of that sense of "inwardness" which is characteristic of the fourth dimension (line 149), as well as that "motion without motion" which is true progression in the direction of the fourth dimension (line 152); also, the succession of cubes moving in a parallel manner away from the physical cube, without diminution in size (line 192–200). When concentrating on this dimension alone, in other words, it was fairly clearly perceived; although, the fact that all four dimensions were not perceived simultaneously, makes this something different from pure four-dimensional perception.

This, however, being Mr. Hodson's first experience with this class of phenomena and this order of thought, it would seem reasonable to suppose that greater familiarity with four-dimensional geometry, and definite training of the mind to "see" four-dimensionally, would have beneficial results in the direction of opening up an apparently dormant sense—the ability to see things "four-square," if I may use the term.[1]

---

[1] Other investigators, it is hoped, may experience the same expansion of consciousness with definite self-training. The chapter on "Mathematics" in my *Theosophy and the Fourth Dimension* is offered as comprising a series of mental gymnastics with this end in view.

2. The second instance wherein the results obtained were not in line with expectations was in the description of the four-dimensional counterpart of the physical cube (Fig. 4). I fully expected a perfect tesseract to be described; a figure, that is, having equal extension in four directions, as illustrated in Fig. 19 of my book. Instead, we obtained a tesseractoid having four-dimensional characteristics, but extending beyond the artificial limitations of an ideal mathematical tesseract.

Upon further reflection, however, it is now clear that the expectation of a perfect tesseract was founded on hastily considered premises. While it is true that a tesseract is the ideal four-dimensional figure corresponding to the cube in the three-dimensional world, it no more follows that every cube should have a tesseract for its superphysical counterpart than that every square should have a cube for its three-dimensional counterpart. As a matter of fact, the square can be a cross-section through a rectangular prism, a pyramid, a triangular prism, and almost any number of complex regular and irregular figures.

Similarly, the cube can form the base of a host of four-dimensional figures, of which the tesseract is the simplest and most perfect, mathematically; but it is not the only one. The puzzling cross-form and the " U " described in the first experiment may have something to do with this fact.

What Mr. Hodson did see, however, has greater significance than what he failed to see—to some sceptical minds, perhaps greater significance *because* he failed to satisfy all expectations.

OBJECTIONS AND DIFFICULTIES

THAT the theory of the fourth dimension bristles with difficulties is not to be denied. Many of them are of a purely technical nature, and vanish when the theory in its many implications is better understood. Others, however, are inherent in the conception itself, and indicate either a weakness in the theory, as it has so far been worked out, or a wrong application of the theory to circumstances it does not properly fit. Stretching a theory beyond its natural limitations will always show up its thin spots, and an honest seeker after truth will never be so wedded to one viewpoint that it will tend to blind him to its inherent limitations or, perhaps, entire falsity.

1. One objection that Mr. Hodson points out to me is in connection with the four-dimensional explanation of the phenomenon of clairvoyant X-ray vision (see Fig. 3). In the two-and-three-dimensional analogy, the translucency of a two-dimensional figure is explained by the raising of the consciousness into three-dimensional space, from which vantage point

every particle of the plane surface is equally visible. However, if every object in this plane has a three-dimensional counterpart, then these counterparts would impede three-dimensional vision, and we would be no better off than before.

This is a difficulty that frankly did not occur to me before, nor do I remember seeing Hinton, Ouspensky, or Claude Bragdon refer to it anywhere. It had me puzzled for a time, till it occurred to me that perhaps I was carrying out an analogy too literally. The mutual relationship between one plane and the next higher, in other words, might be somewhat different once we had gone beyond the three-dimensional world. If this was so, the difficulty Mr. Hodson pointed out as inherent in the two-and-three-dimensional analogy might not apply in three-and-four-dimensional space.

Now, if we begin with the realm of no dimensions, and work up to the realm of three dimensions, we notice an increasing gradation of " solidity " : the line is fuller than the point, the square than the line, and the cube is the most solid of all. Once we have reached physical matter, however, a reversal of the order of solidity appears to take place. We have, first, dense solid matter ; then liquid matter ; then gas ; and finally radio-active emanation and the charged particles—electrons and protons—that constitute the " bricks " out of which matter is made, all in *decreasing* " solidity," and increasing ethereality, if I may use the word.

If we then take the next step, from three-dimensional matter to four-dimensional, we feel that the law of analogy gives us the right to expect a still greater degree of attenuation rather than the reverse: a four-dimensional body would thus be not more solid than a three-dimensional, but less so; and four-dimensional counterparts, stretching out into four-space, would thus not impede four-dimensional vision for this very reason.

With this amplification, the four-dimensional explanation of clairvoyance still holds good, but we have in the meantime learnt one important lesson: the danger of hasty generalization, and the necessity of supplementing theory, wherever possible, with observed fact—a tribute, once more, to the value of such experiments as Mr. Hodson has here been carrying out.[1]

---

[1] Those who have an interest in curious analogies will no doubt be struck by the thought that, in the ascending series above presented, we seem to have a decrease in the number of dimensions properly belonging to the state of matter in question. Thus, the dense solid is three-dimensional; the liquid is, properly, only two-dimensional (since its surface is its only inherent characteristic, its third-dimensional shape being only borrowed, so to speak, from the vessel in which it is contained). A gas, similarly, is one-dimensional: here we have no cohesion

2. Another difficulty that has been mentioned to me arises from the fact that the conception of a four-dimensional object necessitates the assumption that it consists of an infinite number of three-dimensional solids (just as a cube consists of an infinite number of squares). Now a square, being purely a mathematical entity and having no real physical existence, can easily be visualized as having no thickness, thus making an infinite number of such squares understandable, even if it cannot actually be pictured. But with the cube, the case is somewhat different, since we feel that it has physical reality, and the possibility of an infinite number of such cubes becomes inconceivable.

The difficulty, however, is purely empirical. We rely too much upon our physical senses when we say that a cube has independent reality. It is quite easy to conceive—at least theoretically—that a cube is only a cross-section through something far more real; when we have gone thus far, the conception of an infinite number of such cross-sections

---

between particles such as we find in the solid and liquid; gaseous activity consists, on the contrary, in the linear movement of individual molecules. An electron or proton, to pursue the analogy, is a point-charge of electricity—no-dimensional. Then from the no-dimensional world, we jump into the four-dimensional—a paradox.

presents no inherent difficulty, since each cross-section would have no thickness in the four-dimensional direction.

We can even construct an analogy that will correctly picture the above fact, and, since we somehow feel that we do not fully understand a thing until we have pictured it, the attempt may be interesting. A cube, for instance, existing in a certain location between one and two o'clock on a certain day, can be measured in four directions: let us say, one inch wide, one inch deep, one inch high, and one hour long—the word "hour" in this case, of course, only being a contraction for the phrase "a *distance* traversed by consciousness in one hour."

Here we have a definite four-dimensional entity—the tesseract—of which the physical cube is only a cross-section. At any one moment, however, that cube has only three dimensions, since a moment has no length of time, and therefore no thickness in the four-dimensional direction. Just as the time-space of an hour can easily be conceived as containing an infinite number of moments, so can the tesseract be just as easily conceived as consisting of an infinite number of momentary cross-sections, each cross-section taking the form of a cube, representing the momentary appearance of a tesseract.

3. A third difficulty presents itself in the

phenomenon of prevision, for here the question of predetermination and free-will is involved. If we believe with the Behaviourists and some philosophers that every action is definitely predetermined by the entire past of the individual in conjunction with the influence of the environment—in other words, that it is merely a case of stimulus and response—then, evidently, no problem exists. The entire future of an individual can in this case be easily conceived as already existing in another dimension. If, on the other hand, we view every action as freely chosen, then the phenomenon of prevision becomes entirely inexplicable, from the four-dimensional standpoint or any other.

Ouspensky[1] has tried to meet this difficulty by presupposing that at each moment of life an almost endless series of possibilities open themselves up ; the free choice of one of these possibilities brings the individual to the next point in time, at which another multitude of possibilities present themselves, and so on in an endless series.[2] The actual four-dimensional world, he says, contains *all* the possibilities, but just how man makes the choice between one and all the others—and how the clairvoyant can pick out the " possibility " that the man

---

[1] *Tertium Organum.*
[2] Cf. line 721.

is seen to make—remains a mystery, as I have already indicated.[1]

Due to the fragmentary data at present before us exemplifying prevision of the future, it would seem rash to make any definite statements on the subject.[2] A rich field of experimentation opens up before us, as a result of which, perhaps, a more satisfactory understanding of the phenomenon will be secured. If speculation on such a subject is not out of order, I would suggest that man's actions are of two kinds : (1) those that are predetermined by the entire past of the individual, and which constitute a true response of an organism to a certain situation ; and (2) those that are arbitrarily " willed " for no good reason at all. If we then suppose that the clairvoyant sees only the first series (because of the logical connection that exists between one moment and the next), then the difficulty of prevision is easily appreciated, for a large group of actions is thus left out of account, simply because, being arbitrary, it cannot be taken into account. But the difficulty of differentiating between one class of actions and the other from the four-dimensional standpoint still exists. The above suggestion is therefore put forward very hesitatingly, for the thoughts it may provoke

---

[1] Cf. *Theosophy and the Fourth Dimension*, pp. 50–54.

[2] See, however, C. W. Leadbeater, *Devachanic Plane*, p. 14, and *Clairvoyance*, Chapter VII.

rather than for any inherent value it may have in itself.[1]

---

[1] In answer to this line of thought, Mr. Hodson makes the following remarks: "This does not meet the case fully. In prevision there is no uncertainty as of picking out a possibility, or any sense of indeterminance. The action and environment are "seen" and "known." The seer perceives the finished product of the past and the will in actual expression in the future; *i.e.* he does not merely consider which course out of many possible ones will be taken: he only sees the decision carried out in action.

"If some impersonal mode of research could be devised, it might be possible to work all this out by Causal clairvoyance; *i.e.* from the standpoint of egoic vision and prescience."

SUGGESTIONS FOR FURTHER RESEARCH

I BELIEVE that the outstanding value of the preceding series of experiments is not only that it corroborates four-dimensional theory and its relation to astral phenomena, but that it beats out a path for further investigation, for there must be many who are sufficiently endowed with clairvoyant power to carry on where Mr. Hodson has left off and fill in the gaps that are glaringly evident. The direction that this research will take will be sufficiently indicated by a perusal of my other work on the subject, as well as the present; a few points that need clearing up may here be indicated:

1. We have investigated a four-dimensional counterpart of a physical cube, and have also found it possible to explain astral vision four-dimensionally. We may state, therefore (provisionally at least), that astral matter is four-dimensional. The reverse, however, is not necessarily true: Everything four-dimensional is not necessarily astral. To give an example, the four-dimensional counterpart of the physical cube is not necessarily astral in constitution.

Admitting that astral space is four-dimensional, it may be only one of the infinite number of "fourth dimensions" possible, and the superphysical counterpart *may be* an extension into a fourth dimension that is not at all coterminous with astral space. This point needs investigation.

We have also seen that a physical object extends into a four-dimensional space wherein the fourth dimension is represented by our concept Time. Fig. 4 *may be* an extension into the fourth dimension of Time.

It is of course also possible that a cube can have extensions both along the dimension of Time and the dimension comprising astral space, each extension (taken by itself) having the appearance of Fig. 4. In this case, the object in its entirety (combining both physical and astral characteristics) would be five-dimensional, as follows:

1st dimension	. .	in Space
2nd ,,	. .	in Space
3rd ,,	. .	in Space
4th ,,	. .	in Time
5th ,,	. .	Astral.

As has already been explained, either 4 or 5 could be called arbitrarily the "fourth" dimension if the other were temporarily ignored. All five dimensions are at right angles to each other, and, on the basis of such a complicated figure, the cross-form and the "U" previously seen may have some significance.[1]

2. Astral objects should be carefully examined with the view to detecting their four-dimensional character.

3. The remaining platonic solids should be examined, and their super-physical characteristics worked out. (An illustration of the four-dimensional counterpart of the sphere will be found in Johann van Manen's *Some Occult Experiences.*)

4. Four-dimensional "solidity" should be more definitely investigated, in continuation of the first question raised in the Third Experiment.

5. The apparent endlessness of the four-dimensional extension in Fig. 4 would bear closer examination. If the extension described is along the dimensions of Time, the cube conceivably must have a beginning somewhere in the Past and an end somewhere in the Future.

---

[1] In a previous series of experiments, Mr. Hodson had occasion to examine a bar magnet clairvoyantly, describing it partially as follows: "The forces flowing in the centre of the magnet produce a form which resembles a lotus, which increases in dimensional powers (mathematically) plane by plane. . . . At the astral level, this is four-dimensional." Following out the lotus petals into each of the dimensions, he speaks of "geometrical forms of increasing complexity."

6. As regards " prevision," it would be interesting to investigate the question of predestination, in so far as this is physically possible.

REMARKS BY GEOFFREY HODSON

AFTER reading Mr. Horne's reports of, and comments upon, our mutual researches into the fourth dimension, I feel that both an apology and an explanation are due for the obvious limitations on my clairvoyant faculty. I must admit that I found the work very trying and difficult, in spite of Mr. Horne's most sympathetic treat ment of the investigations.

Accuracy in clairvoyant research into geometrical problems demands the ability to exclude all irrelevant phenomena. No non-clairvoyant can possibly appreciate this difficulty. In the first place, as soon as clairvoyant sight is "turned on," one becomes aware of extremely potent discharges of energy from the earth itself, from every object in the room, from one's own body and that of one's colleagues, as well as from the object itself. At first these numerous streams of energy are extremely confusing, and the clairvoyant must in some way develop the technique of self-insulation, both mentally and physically, from their effects.

Again, every atom of these emanations and of all solid substances (and therefore of the object under investigation) contains consciousness as well as energy, and all objects display visibly their whole history to clairvoyant sight.[1] This too has to be excluded in such research as that described in this book.

Another difficulty with which the investigator has to contend is the fact of interplane correspondences which further confuse the investigator and render absolute accuracy extremely difficult to obtain. This universe appears to be constructed on numerical principles, which diagrammatically can be likened to the notes and octaves of the keyboard of a piano. The dense physical world—with its notes of solid, liquid, gaseous and four etheric states—corresponds to the lowest octave. The next world (the emotional) is an octave higher; the mental, higher still; whilst beyond that are four other planes, each subdivided into seven. All of these planes occupy the same actual location and interpenetrate each other.[2]

On the whole, however, interference is prevented by the difference in frequency and

---

[1] That is, they manifest hyper-dimensional characteristics in Time as well as in space. See " Remarks on the Fifth Experiment."—A. H.

[2] [See, however, the mathematical discussion of this " interpenetrating " space of many dimensions, in *Theosophy and the Fourth Dimension*, pp. 64–69.—A. H.]

density between the planes, but there are certain interior correspondences which operate, apparently on the principle of harmonics, by means of which phenomena and states of consciousness appropriate to one plane may osmose into another. Thus it appeared that one of the subplanes of the emotional is in direct correspondence with the plane of abstract mind, so that an object which, with a slightly lower order of vision, appears concrete and limited in time, space, and dimension respectively, may to a slightly higher order of vision appear in terms of abstract existence outside of those limitations. The visions of the " U " and cross shapes associated with the physical cube are, I believe, explainable by means of these interplane relationships.

With regard to the fourth dimension itself, I must admit that I cannot claim ever to have brought clearly into my brain-consciousness a true conception of this added dimension or direction in space. It appears that when the consciousness is translated from one plane to another, privation occurs, so that the realization of that higher condition is lost, though the memory of it may be brought over, translated into terms of the lower. This limitation may be partly overcome by self-training, but I have not yet succeeded in rising above certain apparently inevitable limitations.

From this point of view, therefore, the

clairvoyant investigations are not entirely satisfactory to me, though I feel that my collaborator has treated them most effectively and made good use of the slight material with which I provided him. Mentally, I feel able to say that the fourth dimension could be described as "within-ness" or "throughth," to accept the appropriate word coined by the late W. T. Stead.

APPENDIX

Time and Free-Will in Modern Science

IT is interesting to study Mr. Hodson's experiment with Time in the light of present knowledge in modern science. Two elements are here involved: the relativity of Time, and the determinism of material phenomena.

The former concept is well illustrated in Edington's

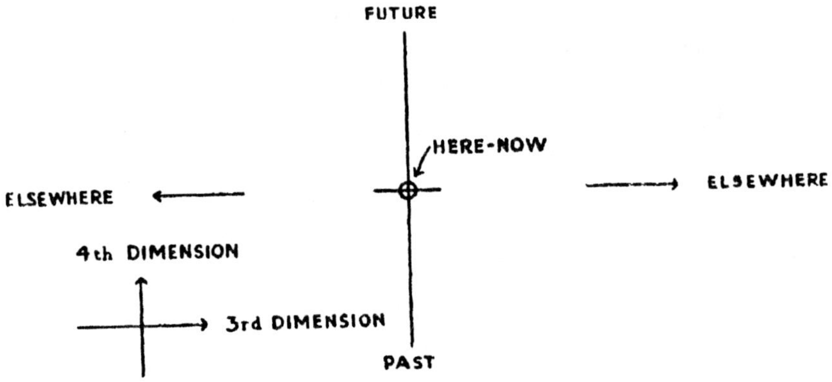

Fig. A

The Nature of the Physical Universe by means of the accompanying diagrams.

In Fig. A the point "Here-Now" denotes the central position occupied by the observer, in this case "myself." To the right and to the left of me stretches the Elsewhere. Before me and behind me are the Future and the Past. Disregarding the other two spatial dimensions for convenience' sake, we may designate right-and-left the Third Dimension, whereat

Future-and-Past (or Time in general) becomes the Fourth.

Surveying the situation from the standpoint of the modern Relativity theory, the fact is borne in upon us that we only know definitely and absolutely that

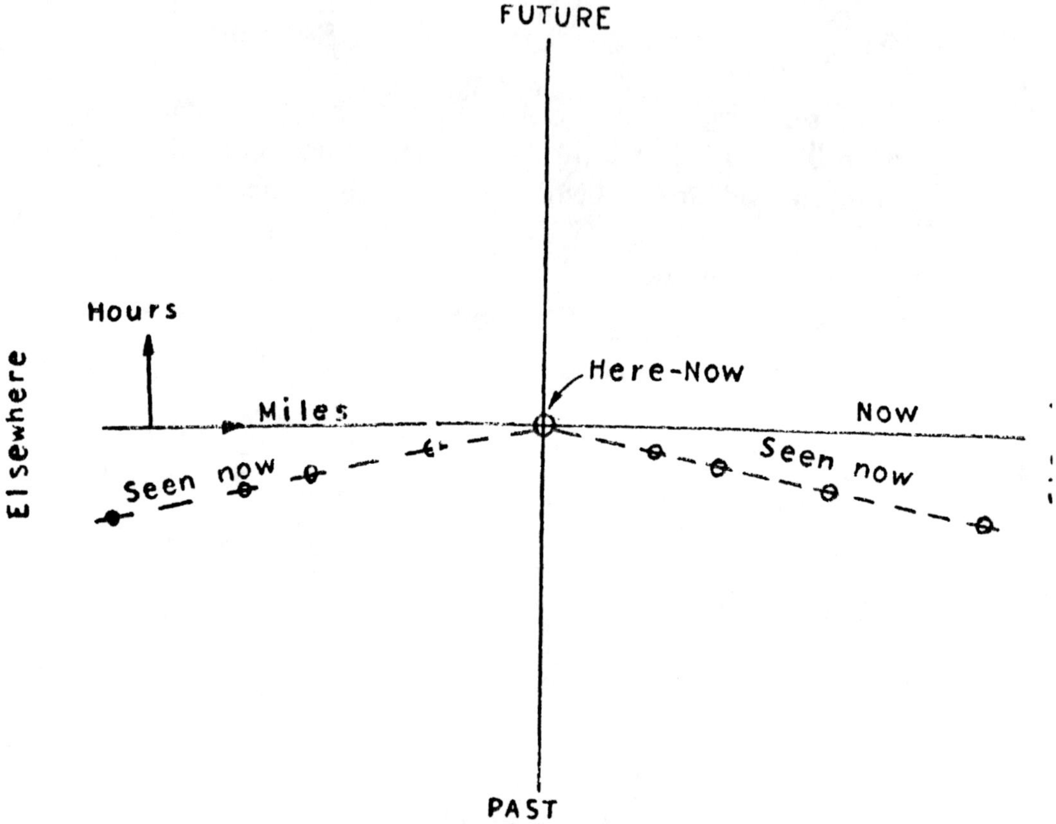

FIG. B

[1] My frame of reference.

which is immediately present to our consciousness, namely, the here and now. Those events, on the other hand, which are far out in space, or are behind or before us in time, are purely relative to our central position here-now, and can only be known inferentially. They, in turn, become known to us definitely and absolutely only when they come to impinge upon our consciousness as the here-now.

To express the proposition more pointedly, we only know " now " in an absolute sense when it is at the same time " here." A " now " which is " elsewhere "

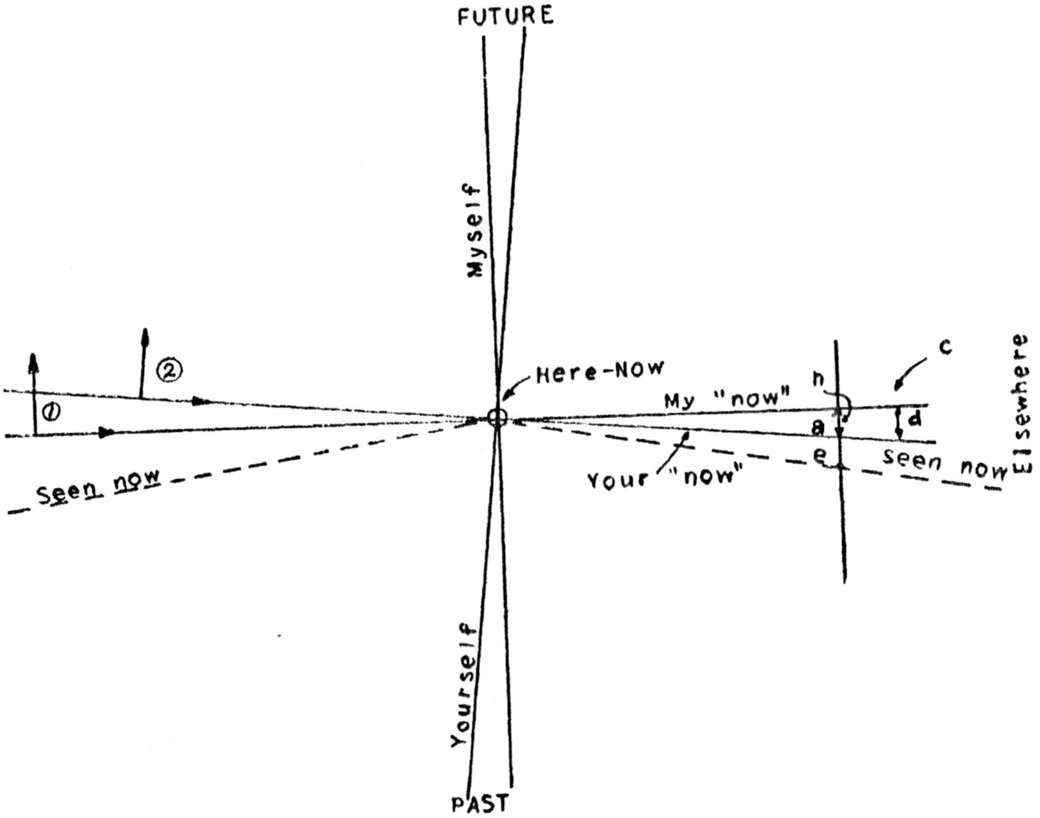

Fig. C

[2] Your frame of reference.

has for us no absolute meaning. It was at one time thought, however, that the word " now " had an absolute meaning of itself, dividing Past from Future with a definiteness that had equal validity in all portions of the universe. In other words, that which occurred at a certain instant, anywhere, was believed to occur simultaneously for all beings, everywhere.

But it was soon found that this conception had to be modified somewhat. Cosmic events could only be apprehended visually—and light takes time to travel. Consequently, that which I see now, out in space, really occurred some time ago; that which is taking place "now," will only enter my consciousness sometime later. Thus a correction has to be made in my picture of the universe, to allow for the sluggishness of light. I can no longer draw an absolute line of world-events through space, separating Past from Future everywhere, and confidently call this line "Now." All I know definitely is that a series of events, taking place at different times on all sides of me, is apprehended by me here and now, and, knowing their location in space, I can plot their respective positions on my diagram. I thus find that they all fall into one line on both sides of me, and these lines (Figs. B and C) I designate as "seen-now." In each case, the horizontal distance between an event and my position "Here-Now" indicates its linear distance from me; the vertical distance indicates the time that has actually elapsed between the event and my seeing it.

From this line "seen-now" I can work backwards, however, and—making due allowance for the speed of light—I construct the line "Now" to represent my cleavage between Past and Future as regards all world-events taking place out in space. This line "Now," of course, can also be conveniently used to represent the instantaneous line of world-events for every human being on our little speck of a globe. In other words, my

" now " is your " now," and there is so far no conflict.

When we take cosmic events on a larger scale, however, a disturbing discrepancy creeps in. Suppose you, for instance, instead of being on this globe with me, were on a comet, travelling at a different rate of speed. Let us imagine further that at the moment under discussion, our two positions approach close enough in the scale of stellar distances to be considered as occupying the same space. My " Here-Now " then becomes your " Here-Now," and we can thus start plotting our world-lines from the same central point of reference (Fig. C).

Since we see the same cosmic events at the same time, our respective " Seen now " lines coincide and overlap one another. When you, however, come to work backwards (as I had already done in Fig. B) from your " Seen now " line to your " now " line, you find strangely enough that it does not coincide with mine. Due to the difference in our respective speeds, something has happened to our units of measurement (the famous Fitzgerald contraction), and—in making allowance for your speed of light[1]—you find that what is " now " to you, far out in space, is not at all " now " to me, however difficult it may be for us to visualize such a strange fact. If you examine Fig. C, you will readily see that an event *a* which, according to your frame of reference, is occurring " now," has already occurred, as far as I am concerned, *b* hours ago. Yet, when actual sight of the event reaches our eyes, it will be

[1] Numerically the same as, but actually different from, mine, since different yard-sticks are used.

seen by both of us simultaneously, and will correspond to the seen event *e*. Conversely, another event *c*, which is occurring in my universe "now," is still ahead of you in time by a space of *d* hours. As far as you are concerned, it has not yet occurred. To make matters worse, there is absolutely no way of determining which of us is right, since a third party, with a frame of reference all his own, would differ from both of us. We therefore compromise by saying that both of us are correct as far as our respective frames of reference are concerned—the word "now" has now become purely relative, and the concept of simultaneity has lost all its absolute meaning.

The Past and Future of the *same* event are thus interchangeable, and while in the past we thought we knew something definite of the Present, we have now come to realize that we do not definitely know anything even of the Now. Such is the paradoxical situation presented to us seriously and in all sincerity by the most abstruse of modern sciences.

When Time is shown to be so purely relative, and the Present is shorn of all its absolute quality, we can afford to give more serious consideration to such conceptions as are put before us in Mr. Hodson's investigations. To translate psychometry (whether of the past or future) into Relativity terms, we might say that the art of the clairvoyant consists "merely" in transferring his consciousness to a frame of reference in which the past or future event in question is occurring "now." If at the same time a clairvoyance-in-space be conveniently assumed, so that "now" becomes "here-now," all difficulties—presto !—

vanish. (The actual physical conditions that would make the necessary transference feasible might be beyond the bounds of probability, without destroying the value of the picture thus vividly presented to our understanding.)[1]

---

[1] Many years ago a writer tried to illustrate the Eternal Now in God's consciousness by recourse to the phenomenon of light-travel. At a distance of one light-year, said he (5,850,000,000,000 miles), an entity viewing the events on earth would actually see only those which took place a year ago. At an appropriately greater distance away, events further back in time would appear before him. Conversely, the events of to-day will be taking place " now " to an entity a million years hence, provided his point of consciousness were a million light-years away. Granting to God an all-embracing consciousness, capable of filling all points in space, the entire Past becomes to the mind of God a static and eternal Present.

The picture of course is a graphic one and easily visualized, but there its value ends. Aside from the fact that only events out in the open, in cloudless daylight, would be capable of traversing space—an annoying limitation to the divine vision—a more serious difficulty lies in the fact that only the Past becomes the Present; the Future remains where it is. Curiously enough, Maeterlinck, in his *Life of Space*, succumbs to the same error.

H. G. Wells has made a rather more scientific attempt at bringing both Past and Future within the ken of the Present. In *The Time Machine* he has made one of his characters invent a contrivance that can propel a person in either temporal direction with controllable speed: forwards a million years to view an event—backwards a like space of time to tell the tale. Granting this idea the serious consideration due all scientific romances (since so many of them have already turned out to have been

APPENDIX

A difficulty inherent in the theory of Time as a fourth dimension of space must now be discussed. The Relativists speak of a four-dimensional continuum, and we have here spoken of a four-dimensional extension in space, of which the fourth represents that which to our limited consciousness appears under the guise of Time. There are certain difficulties in this conception that cannot be ignored.

---

visions of things to come), we yet find one inherent difficulty :

A proper and legitimate acceleration of time is that shown us by a speeded-up motion-picture. Thus, the entire life of a plant from birth to death can be depicted in half a minute or less. Every detail in the life of that plant is correctly reproduced, and no event is seen in an accelerated picture that does not actually occur in real life.

In the "time journey," however, one discrepancy occurs—the existence of the traveller: an illegitimate projection into the future of something that in the future will not (or "does not") exist. On the other hand, allowing for the possibility of reincarnation (or the possibility of looking down from some heavenly plane, if one prefers to be orthodox), then the time-traveller would see himself either as a true member of the future humanity, or as a denizen of this superphysical sphere—in either case something different from the traveller in his present physical body.

One thing is certain. No time-machine, no hypnotic technique as in the experiments of de Rochas, could ever be devised on the basis of the materialistic theory. On this theory, granting the possibility of an acceleration in consciousness, running ahead of Father Time himself, one would finally come to the end of mortal life, and the consequent extinction of the time-traveller. How he would then make his way back to life to tell the tale I will leave it to my readers to puzzle out.

APPENDIX

Now a *static* four-dimensional space and a consciousness functioning four-dimensionally therein is a simple enough situation. To such a consciousness, Time need have no existence, since all things are eternally and unchangeably co-present. To such a consciousness, for instance, our physical universe could exist as one of an infinite number of three-dimensional " planes " eternally stretched out in the direction of the fourth dimension. In such a world-picture, the notion of Time is nowhere involved.

Our universe, however, is not static. It moves ; it grows ; it changes. To account for this change, to account for our perception of time-sequence, we say that, within this static four-dimensional universe, our three-dimensional " plane of consciousness " is *moving* in the direction of the fourth dimension, each cross-section representing a momentary glimpse of the whole, appearing in our minds now in one form and now in another. However, as soon as we introduce this *motion,* though it be only of consciousness, the problem of Time reasserts itself, since without Time no motion is conceivable. We are thus faced by the tantalizing Sphinx again. The only escape possible from this enigma is by asserting, with the Idealists, that this motion of consciousness is itself an illusion, and there is no real motion at all, not even in consciousness. Life, then, is a dream ; and in this dream we dream that we dream. The Christian Scientists and, before them, the Vedantins, have indeed attempted to cut this Gordian knot by postulating that even the dream-within-the-dream does not exist. But while Life is thus simply explained away, Life goes merrily on.

The application of four-dimensional conceptions to

the question of Time is thus not quite so simple as at first blush appears, and it may well be that the entire concept (in this respect at least) is fallacious, however valid it may be in other departments of thought. It may indeed be that we super-geometricians are merely applying, Nelson-like, the blind eye to the telescope. Time is not only an elusive, but may after all be an entirely independent category.

W. Whately Smith, in his chapter on "Time and Prevision," points out that Bergson differentiates between the time "of succession" and the time "of duration," and that the succession of events by which we *measure* time "no more *is* time than the succession of markers on a foot-rule *is* the material which we measure with it." Smith himself inclines to the view that there is a physical time pertaining to three-space, marked by changes in this three-space world, and another time expressing changes in the four-space world. While the former variety of time is expressible in four-dimensional terms, the latter variety requires five dimensions.

This *may* be the way out of our perplexity. Motion in a four-dimensional Space-Time continuum would then have to be conceived five-dimensionally; motion in this five-dimensional continuum, six-dimensionally. What is Time to us would be Space to a four-dimensional being; what is Time to him would be Space to a five-dimensional being. And so on in an infinite series till we reach the Absolute Consciousness itself, in which alone there is no time, no motion (which some say is equivalent to infinite motion); only eternal changelessness. This may after all be the sole Reality.

Going on to the discussion of prevision, Smith

discounts the theory held by some that the future is merely the inevitable outcome of present forces, and that prevision is merely the heightening of a normal faculty, the power to follow in imagination the logical concatenation of events. If such merely were the case, " the accuracy of such a forecast would depend on the perception of *all* the factors involved, as well as on the precision of the unconscious reasoning."

He inclines, therefore, to the belief already expressed above, that the future exists *now*, but this, he thinks, does not imply fatalism. In his two-space analogy, he sees events in the shape of threads stretched out three-dimensionally, cutting the two-dimensional plane in points which, to two-space beings, become physical " things." In the motion of this two-dimensional plane in the direction of Time, he believes that " two-space beings might be able to alter the arrangement of the threads during their passage across the film. . . ." Thus, free-will is restored in a universe apparently rigid.

An error, however, creeps into the argument at this point, I think. So long as we conceive of a rigid thread-filled universe, we are on comparatively safe ground. As soon as we introduce the possibility of a lateral change in the position of any one of these threads, we introduce a motion in an impossible direction, since we have postulated in the beginning that time-motion takes place perpendicular—not parallel—to the plane.

On the question of free-will, the latest discoveries in modern science point to some very interesting conclusions, reversing the doctrine of absolute determinism which has played such a prominent part in the philosophy of physical and chemical science up till comparatively recent times. Thus, it has hitherto been believed that, given a definite physical force, and the conditions under which it was acting, a definite result would obtain, reproducible absolutely and identically a million times over. The belief soon became axiomatic, Biology and Physiology joining the procession, with the various " mechanisms " intended to explain and describe the supposedly deterministic processes of the organism. Still more recently, Psychology has come into the fold, and in Behaviourism attempts to show the rigid determinism of mental and volitional processes.

It is to be noted, however, that in Biology already, the idea of a mechanistic basis of life has been definitely left behind by many of the leading scientists.[1] The " mechanisms " of the most vital functions—despite decades of painstaking research and the utmost refinements in technique—have not yet been discovered, and, in the opinion of these scientists, are not discoverable, because they cannot conceivably exist. In Psychology, however, we still hear discussions of " why we behave like " this and that, but Edington gravely warns the Psychologists that if any determinism is to be proven in psychic life, the problem must be attacked from the standpoint of the mental process itself, apart from any analogy with physical determinism.

For in Physics, strange to say, scientists have of late begun to doubt the validity of their previously reared scaffolding of rigid determinism. " There are others beside myself," asserts Edington, " who have recently begun to question it "[2]—though, in the

[1] See J. B. S. Haldane, *Mechanism, Life, and Personality.*
[2] *Op. cit.*

mechanical structure of the universe, one would concede, rigid determinism is logical enough, and far easier to conceive than its absence.

Jeans, however, points out in *The Mysterious Universe* that the notion of determinism and causation in mechanical law is true only in the average; in individual cases there is a loose-jointedness that Heisenberg calls the "principle of indeterminacy," and Dirac has gone so far as to say that if an experiment were repeated several times under *precisely* the same conditions, several different results might be obtained.

Since the law of strict causation has been thus destroyed, says Jeans, the result is that, up to the present at least, "the picture of the universe presented by the new physics contains more room than did the old mechanical picture for life and consciousness to exist within the picture itself, together with the attributes which we commonly associate with them, such as free-will. . . ."

Edington goes further. The future of any event, he says, "is a combination of the causal influences of the past together with unpredictable elements. . . . Science therefore withdraws its moral opposition to free-will." Taking a dig at the Behaviourists, he points out elsewhere that "it is meaningless to say that the behaviour of a conscious brain is precisely the same as that of a mechanical brain if the behaviour of a mechanical brain is left undetermined. If the laws of physics are not strictly causal, the most that can be said is that the behaviour of the conscious brain is one of the possible behaviours of a mechanical brain. Precisely so; and the decision between the possible behaviours is what we call volition."

APPENDIX

Hearkening back to the Relativity theory, we are left free to accept the possibility of Prevision, on the basis of a projection of consciousness on to a frame of reference wherein the " future " becomes the " now " and the volitional choice between alternate lines of behaviour is actually seen being made.

BIBLIOGRAPHY

On the Fourth Dimension:

Hinton, *The Fourth Dimension.*

Ouspensky, *Tertium Organum.*

Claude Bragdon, *A Primer of Higher Space*, and *Four-dimensional Vistas.*

Horne, *Theosophy and the Fourth Dimension.*

W. Whately Smith, *A Theory of the Mechanism of Survival.*

Richard Eriksen, *Consciousness, Life, and the Fourth Dimension.*

On Occult Phenomena:

Leadbeater, *The Astral Plane, The Devachanic Plane,* and *Man, Visible and Invisible.*

Besant, *The Ancient Wisdom*, and *Man and his Bodies.*

Johann van Manen, *Some Occult Experiences.*

Hodson, *The Science of Seership.*

Blavatsky, *The Secret Doctrine*, 3rd. Edition, vol. I, pp. 38, 44, 69, 271, 295, 450, 662, 675, 734.

On Relativity:

Slosson, *Easy Lessons in Einstein.*

Coode Adams, *A Primer of Occult Physics.*

Nordmann, *Einstein and the Universe.*

Edington, *The Nature of the Physical World.*

Printed in the United States
919600001B